Contents

Introduction

The contents of this book are based upon the National Science Education Standards for Grade 7. These standards include (A) Science as Inquiry, (B) Physical Science, (C) Life Science, (D) Earth and Space Science, (E) Science and Technology, (F) Science in Personal and Social Perspectives, and (G) History and Nature of Science.

This book will help teachers, students, parents, and tutors. Teachers can use this book either to introduce or review a topic in their science classroom. Students will find the book useful in reviewing the major concepts in science. Parents can use this book to help their children with topics that may be posing a problem in the classroom. Tutors can use this book as a basis for their lessons and for assigning questions and activities.

This book includes ten lessons that focus on the ten major concepts presented in the content standards: Physical Science, Life Science, and Earth and Space Science. The lessons also cover the twelve major concepts presented in the other standards. A table on page 4 provides a correlation between the contents of each lesson and the National Science Education Standards.

Before beginning the book, the reader can check his or her knowledge of the content by completing the *Assessment*. The *Assessment* consists of questions that deal with the content standards. This will allow the reader to determine how much he or she knows about a particular concept before beginning to read about it. The *Assessment* may also serve as a way of leading the reader to a specific lesson that may be of special interest.

Each lesson follows the same sequence in presenting the material. A list of *Key Terms* is always provided at the beginning of each lesson. This list includes all the boldfaced terms and their definitions presented in the same order that they are introduced in the lesson. The reader can develop a sense of the lesson content by glancing through the *Key Terms*. Each lesson then provides background information about the concept. This information is divided into several sections. Each section is written so that the reader is not overwhelmed with details. Rather, the reader is guided through the concept in a logical sequence. Each lesson then moves on to a *Review*. This section consists of several multiple-choice and short-answer questions. The multiple-choice questions check if the reader has retained information that was covered in the lesson. The short-answer questions check if the reader can use information from the lesson to provide the answers.

Each lesson then moves on to a series of activities. These activities are designed to check the reader's understanding of the information. Some activities extend the lesson by presenting additional information. The activities are varied so as not to be boring. For example, reading passages about interesting and unusual findings are included. Questions to check reading comprehension are then asked. As a change of pace, some activities are meant to engage the reader in a "fun-type" exercise. These activities include crosswords, word searches, jumbled letters, and cryptograms.

The last activity in each lesson is an experiment. Each experiment has been designed so that the required items are easy to locate and can usually be found in most households. Care has been taken to avoid the use of any dangerous materials or chemicals. However, an adult should always be present when a student is conducting an experiment. In some cases, the experimental procedure reminds students that adult supervision is required. Before beginning any experiment, an adult should review the list of materials and the procedure. In this way, the adult will be aware of any situations that may need special attention. The adult should review the safety issues before the experiment is begun. The adult may want to check a laboratory manual for specific safety precautions that should be followed when doing an experiment, such as wearing safety goggles and never touching or tasting chemicals.

The book then follows with a *Science Fair* section. Information is presented on how to conduct and present a science fair project. In some cases, the experiment at the end of a lesson can serve as the basis for a science fair project. Additional suggestions are also provided with advice as to how to choose an award-winning science fair project.

A *Glossary* is next. This section lists all the boldfaced terms in alphabetical order and indicates the page on which the term is used. The book concludes with an *Answer Key*, which gives the answers to all the activity questions, including the experiment.

This book has been designed and written so that teachers, students, parents, and tutors will find it easy to use and follow. Most importantly, students will benefit from this book by achieving at a higher level in class and on standardized tests.

National Science Education Standards

Standard A: SCIENCE AS INQUIRY

A1 Abilities necessary to do scientific inquiry
A2 Understandings about scientific inquiry

Standard B: PHYSICAL SCIENCE

B1 Properties and changes of properties in matter
B2 Motions and forces
B3 Transfer of energy

Standard C: LIFE SCIENCE

C1 Structure and function in living systems
C2 Reproduction and heredity
C3 Regulation and behavior
C4 Populations and ecosystems
C5 Diversity and adaptations of organisms

Standard D: EARTH AND SPACE SCIENCE

D1 Earth's history and structure
D2 Earth in the solar system

Standard E: SCIENCE AND TECHNOLOGY

E1 Abilities of technological design
E2 Understandings about science and technology

Standard F: SCIENCE IN PERSONAL AND SOCIAL PERSPECTIVES

F1 Personal health
F2 Populations, resources, and environments
F3 Natural hazards
F4 Risks and benefits
F5 Science and technology in society

Standard G: HISTORY AND NATURE OF SCIENCE

G1 Science as a human endeavor
G2 Nature of science
G3 History of science

Correlation to National Science Education Standards

Unit 1: Physical Science

Lesson 1: Properties and Changes of Properties in Matter

Background Information B1, G1, G3
Review B1
Atoms and Elements B1
Compounds and Mixtures B1
Pain Relievers B1, E1, E2, F1, F5, G1, G2, G3
Experiment: Separating the Components
  in a Mixture A1, A2, B1

Lesson 2: Motions and Forces

Background Information B2, E2
Review B2, F5
Speed, Velocity, and Acceleration. B2
Motions and Forces Crossword Puzzle B2
Problem Solving B2
Experiment: Comparing Momentums. . . . A1, A2, B2

Lesson 3: Transfer of Energy

Background Information B3, E2, F1, F3, F4, F5
Review B3, E2, F1, F4, F5, G2
Glowing Meat B3, F1, F3, G1
The Speed of Light B3, D3
Reflection, Refraction, and Absorption. B3, F2
Experiment: Pouring Light A1, A2, B3

Unit 2: Life Science

Lesson 4: Structure and Function in Living Systems

Background Information. C1
Review C1
Ulcers C1, F1, F4, G3
The Circulatory System. C1
Experiment: The Digestive System . . A1, A2, B1, C1

Lesson 5: Reproduction and Heredity

Background Information. C2
Review C2
A Hidden Message C2, G3
A Punnett Square C2
Sickle Cell Anemia. C2, F1, F2
Experiment: Making a Pedigree A1, A2, C2, G1

Lesson 6: Regulation and Behavior

Background Information. C3
Review C3
How Hot Can It Get?. C3, G1, G3
Blood Sugar Levels. C3, F1
Experiment: Perspiration A1, A2, C3

Lesson 7: Populations and Ecosystems

Background Information C4, F2
Review. C4, F2
Biomes of Australia C4, F2
Deep Below the Surface . . C4, F3, F4, F5, G1, G2, G3
Precipitation in a Biome C4, F2
Experiment: Making a
  Balanced Ecosystem A1, A2, C4, F2

Lesson 8: Diversity and Adaptations of Organisms

Background Information C5, E2
Review C5
A Common Ancestor C5
Humans and Apes C5
Primates C5
Comparing Hemoglobin C5, E2
Experiment: Extracting DNA A1, A2, C5

Unit 3: Earth and Space Science

Lesson 9: Earth's History and Structure

Background Information D1, E1, E2, F2, F5
Review D1, E2, F2, F5
Complete the Sentences D1, E2, F2, F5
Drinking Water D1, F2
Energy Resources. D1, F2
If It's Saturday, It Must Be
  Pizza Night D1, E1, E2, F1, F2, F5
Experiment: Hydroelectric Power . A1, A2, E1, E2, F5

Lesson 10: Earth in the Solar System

Background Information D2, G3
Review D2
Velocity in Space D2
Be a Weather Forecaster D2, E1, E2, F5
Tornadoes D2, F3
Earth Crossword Puzzle D2
Experiment: Forecasting
  the Weather A1, A2, D2, E2

Assessment

Darken the circle by the best answer.

1. How are the elements arranged on a periodic table?
   - (A) in alphabetical order
   - (B) by increasing atomic mass
   - (C) by increasing atomic number
   - (D) by increasing atomic size

2. What two factors must be known to determine the velocity of an object in motion?
   - (A) mass and acceleration
   - (B) speed and direction
   - (C) force and mass
   - (D) distance and acceleration

3. Which of the following has the greatest momentum?
   - (A) a basketball player running down court
   - (B) a car traveling down a highway
   - (C) a child learning how to ride a bicycle
   - (D) a jet plane taking off

4. Which of the following statements is true?
   - (A) All electromagnetic waves are invisible.
   - (B) The longer the wavelength of light, the less energy it has.
   - (C) Ultraviolet rays are always dangerous and harmful.
   - (D) Darker colors absorb less compared to lighter colors.

5. A bone is connected to another bone by a(n)
   - (A) joint.
   - (B) ligament.
   - (C) tendon.
   - (D) epiglottis.

6. Blood returning to the heart from all parts of the body except the lungs enters the
   - (A) right atrium.
   - (B) right ventricle.
   - (C) left atrium.
   - (D) left ventricle.

7. For certain guinea pigs, black fur (B) is dominant over brown (b) fur. What can the genotypes be for a guinea pig with black fur?
   - (A) B or b
   - (B) BB or bb
   - (C) Bb or bb
   - (D) BB or Bb

8. A Punnett square is used to
   - (A) determine the phenotype of an organism.
   - (B) see all the possible types of offspring that can be produced.
   - (C) change the genetic makeup of an organism.
   - (D) study the DNA in an organism's chromosomes.

Assessment, page 2

9. Diabetes is caused by
   - (A) a loss of liver function.
   - (B) damage to the nervous system.
   - (C) a hormonal imbalance.
   - (D) negative feedback control.

10. Which of the following is controlled by the medulla?
    - (A) reasoning
    - (B) speech
    - (C) muscle coordination
    - (D) reflex actions

11. Which term includes all the other terms?
    - (A) organism
    - (B) community
    - (C) species
    - (D) ecosystem

12. Which two individuals are likely to have the greatest differences in their DNA?
    - (A) two different breeds of dogs
    - (B) a tiger and a house cat
    - (C) a cat and a dog
    - (D) a tiger and a leopard

13. Which is an example of using a nonrenewable resource?
    - (A) using a wood-burning stove
    - (B) toasting marshmallows over a campfire
    - (C) using a coal-burning stove
    - (D) using a solar-powered calculator

14. Geothermal power comes from
    - (A) heat within Earth.
    - (B) the sun.
    - (C) energy provided by falling water.
    - (D) gasoline.

15. In which layer of Earth are the least dense elements located?
    - (A) crust
    - (B) mantle
    - (C) outer core
    - (D) inner core

16. What gas does photosynthesis add to the atmosphere?
    - (A) carbon dioxide
    - (B) nitrogen
    - (C) ammonia
    - (D) oxygen

Lesson 1 Properties and Changes of Properties in Matter

The ancient Greeks believed that everything they saw could be divided into four categories, which they called "roots." These four roots are also known as elements and include earth, fire, water, and air. The ancient Greeks also believed that everything they saw was composed of very tiny particles. These particles were called atoms. The word *atom* comes from the Greek word *atomos*, which means indivisible. The Greeks believed that these tiny particles were indestructible and came in an infinite variety of shapes and sizes. As you will learn in this lesson, elements and atoms have very different meanings to scientists today than they did to the Greeks over 2000 years ago.

Matter and Atoms

Everything the Greeks saw and everything that you see today is made of matter. **Matter** is anything that has both volume and mass. **Volume** is the amount of space that is taken up, or occupied, by an object. For example, the volume of this book is the amount of space it takes up on a bookshelf or in your backpack.

Key Terms

matter—anything that has both volume and mass

volume—the amount of space taken up, or occupied, by an object

mass—the amount of matter in an object

atom—the basic building block of matter; the smallest unit of an element that maintains the properties of that element

proton—a particle with a positive charge located in the nucleus of an atom

neutron—a neutral particle located in the nucleus of an atom

electron—a particle with a negative charge that moves around the nucleus of an atom

nucleus—the central part of an atom made up of protons and neutrons

element—a substance that cannot be easily changed into another substance

periodic table—an arrangement of the elements so that certain similarities appear at regular intervals

atomic number—the number of protons an element has

group—a column of elements in the periodic table

period—a row of elements in the periodic table

compound—a substance that is made from two or more elements that are chemically combined or bonded

chemical formula—a shorthand method that uses the chemical symbols of elements and numbers to represent a compound

mixture—a blend of two or more substances, each of which retains its own identity

Mass is the amount of matter in an object. Because it has more pages, the mass of a dictionary is greater than the mass of this book.

All matter is made up of atoms. An **atom** can be defined as the basic building block of matter. Contrary to what the Greeks believed, an atom is made up of even smaller particles. Atoms consist of particles known as protons, neutrons, and electrons. A **proton** is a particle with a positive charge. A **neutron** is neutral, meaning that it does not have a charge. An **electron** has a negative charge. Protons and neutrons make up the central core, or **nucleus**, of an atom. Electrons move around the nucleus in regions known as electron clouds.

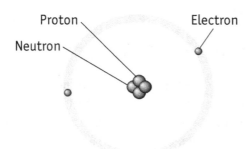

Elements

Recall that the Greeks believed that matter consisted of four elements—earth, fire, water, and air. Today, scientists know that matter consists of 114 known elements, with new elements still being discovered. Scientists define an **element** as any substance that cannot be easily changed into another substance. To change an element into another substance requires a tremendous amount of energy, such as the amount of energy that is released when a nuclear bomb explodes.

Based on the definition of an element, an atom can be defined in another way. An atom can also be defined as the smallest unit of an element that maintains the properties of that element.

The 114 elements that have been discovered are the building blocks of all matter. How can so many forms of matter be made from only 114 elements? Just think about the English alphabet. The 26 letters of the alphabet can be combined and arranged to form all the words that make up the English language. Just imagine how many forms of matter can be made from 114 elements!

The elements are divided into two major groups. One group consists of naturally occurring elements. These elements can be found in nature, either here on Earth or somewhere in the universe. There are 93 naturally occurring elements. Three of these elements are not found on Earth but exist elsewhere in the universe. The second group of elements includes the synthetic elements. These elements cannot be found in nature and are made by scientists in a laboratory. There are 21 synthetic elements. Each element is written as a chemical symbol that consists either of one, two, or three letters.

Examples of natural and synthetic elements	
Natural elements	**Synthetic elements**
Oxygen (O)	Plutonium (Pu)
Hydrogen (H)	Americium (Am)
Copper (Cu)	Californium (Cf)
Lead (Pb)	Einsteinium (Es)
Gold (Au)	Nobelium (No)

The Periodic Table

In 1860, only about 60 elements had been discovered. At that time, a Russian schoolteacher named Dmitri Mendeleev attempted to discover a pattern in these elements. Mendeleev wrote each element's name and properties on a separate card. He then tried to arrange the cards in a pattern.

Mendeleev discovered that when he arranged the known elements, those with similar properties ended up in the same column. This arrangement of the elements was the first step in creating an incredibly useful scientific tool known as the periodic table.

The **periodic table** is an arrangement of the elements so that certain similarities appear at regular intervals. Think of the elements in the periodic table as if they were a set of baseball cards for the starting players of different teams. Suppose that you take all of the cards from one team and place them in a row.

www.harcourtschoolsupply.com
8
Lesson 1, Properties and Changes of Properties in Matter
Science 7, SV 9781419034350

A Periodic Table of the Elements

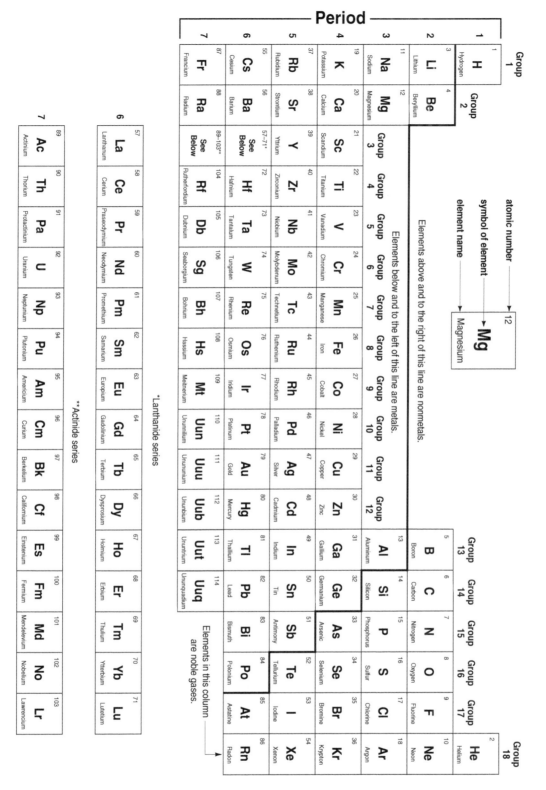

Then you create a second row that contains all of the cards from another team in the same order as the first row. If you continue this pattern for all of the teams, you will have many rows of cards and all of the cards in each column will share a similar feature. All of the catchers will be in one column and all of the pitchers will be in another column. This pattern will help you compare the players for each team.

After Mendeleev created his periodic table, he noticed that a few elements were out of place. In 1911, an English scientist named Henry Moseley solved this problem. Moseley arranged the elements in the periodic table according to their atomic number, not the way Mendeleev had done. An element's **atomic number** corresponds to the number of protons the element has. For example, hydrogen has 1 proton. Therefore, hydrogen's atomic number is 1.

Moseley arranged the elements in order of increasing atomic numbers. He placed hydrogen first in the periodic table. Because helium's atomic number is 2, Moseley placed helium after hydrogen. This pattern is continued for all of the 114 elements in the modern periodic table.

The periodic table is divided into columns and rows. Each column is called a **group** and each row is called a **period**. The periodic table is organized so that you can easily identify elements that share certain properties. All the elements in Group 1 are highly reactive. If these elements are added to water, a violent reaction will occur. In contrast, the elements in Group 18 do not react unless an enormous amount of energy is supplied.

Compounds

Elements can combine or bond with one another to form a compound. A **compound** is a substance that is made from two or more elements that are chemically combined or bonded. Water is one of the most familiar examples of a compound. Water is made of two elements, hydrogen and oxygen. In water, the hydrogen and oxygen are bonded to one another.

The chemical formula for water is H_2O. A **chemical formula** is a shorthand method that uses the chemical symbols of elements and numbers to represent a compound. H represents the chemical symbol for

hydrogen. O represents the chemical symbol for oxygen. The 2 in the formula H_2O indicates that water is made of 2 H atoms and 1 O atom. Notice that the number 1 is never written in a formula.

Hydrogen and oxygen atoms can combine in many other ways. Two hydrogen atoms can combine with two oxygen atoms. In this case, the formula for the compound they produce is written as H_2O_2. Notice that the numbers indicate that 2 hydrogen atoms combine or bond with 2 oxygen atoms. The formula H_2O_2 represents a compound called hydrogen peroxide. Hydrogen peroxide is used for cleaning cuts and scratches to prevent infection.

Oxygen atoms can also form compounds with carbon atoms. Carbon dioxide is an example of a compound that is formed from oxygen and carbon. The formula for carbon dioxide is CO_2. You exhale the CO_2 that is produced in your body during cell respiration. Oxygen and carbon can also bond to form carbon monoxide, CO. Unlike CO_2, CO is poisonous and can cause serious injury or death if it is inhaled. Removing one oxygen atom from CO_2 can make a huge difference!

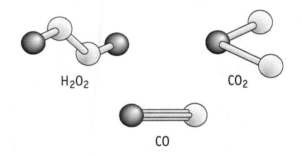

H_2O_2 CO_2

CO

Mixtures

Elements can also form mixtures. A **mixture** is defined as a blend of two or more substances, each of which retains its own identity. You may have eaten a mixture for breakfast. Cereal is an example of a mixture because cereal is a blend of many different distinct substances. Cereal may contain bran flakes, nuts, fruits, and milk. If you wanted to, you could separate these components from cereal. Air is another example of a mixture. Air is a mixture of many gases, including oxygen, nitrogen, and carbon dioxide.

Like elements, mixtures can be natural or synthetic. Minerals are examples of natural mixtures. A mineral called vanadanite is a mixture of the elements vanadium and lead. Mixtures can also be synthetic. For example, stainless steel is made by mixing iron with various other elements such as carbon, chromium, and nickel. Stainless steel is used to make various consumer products, including cookware and kitchen utensils.

Mixtures versus Compounds

Mixtures differ from compounds in several ways. In a compound, the ratio of the elements is always fixed. Recall that the ratio of hydrogen to oxygen in water is always 2:1. In a mixture, the ratio of the components can vary. For example, granite is a mixture of three minerals. Granite comes in different colors, depending on the ratios of these minerals.

A compound has properties that differ from the elements that form it. Sodium is an element that reacts violently with water. Chlorine is an element that is poisonous. However, when sodium combines with chlorine, the compound they form is called sodium chloride, or table salt. In a mixture, each component retains its identity. The three minerals that make up granite each retain their original properties.

The elements that make up a compound can be separated only by using energy. Electrical energy can be used to separate the two elements, hydrogen and oxygen, that make up water. In a mixture, the components can be separated more easily. If you do not like nuts in your cereal, you can just pick them out. However, not all mixtures are as easy to separate into their components. For example, separating the elements in stainless steel involves more effort.

Lesson 1   Review

Darken the circle by the best answer.

1. Which of the following is a definition of an element?

Ⓐ An element is a natural substance that can be used to build matter.

Ⓑ An element is a substance that cannot be easily changed into another substance.

Ⓒ An element is a substance that can be found <u>only</u> in mixtures.

Ⓓ An element is a substance that can be made <u>only</u> by humans.

2. Which of the following represents a compound?

Ⓐ O

Ⓑ O_2

Ⓒ O_3

Ⓓ CO_2

3. How many elements are listed in the periodic table?

Ⓐ 60

Ⓑ 72

Ⓒ 93

Ⓓ 114

4. Which of the following compounds contains the greatest number of <u>different</u> elements?

Ⓐ CO_2

Ⓑ $C_{22}H_{46}$

Ⓒ $C_6H_{12}O_6$

Ⓓ CH_4

5. Examine the following table.

Element	Atomic number
Oxygen	8
Carbon	6
Gold	79
Calcium	40

Which of these four elements is listed first on the periodic table?

Ⓐ oxygen

Ⓑ carbon

Ⓒ gold

Ⓓ calcium

6. Which of the following compounds contains the largest number of atoms?

Ⓐ CO_2

Ⓑ $C_{22}H_{46}$

Ⓒ $C_6H_{12}O_6$

Ⓓ CH_4

7. The elements that make up a compound

Ⓐ are always present in a fixed ratio.

Ⓑ can be easily separated.

Ⓒ retain their original properties.

Ⓓ must always be present in a 2:1 ratio.

Review (cont'd.)

8. Explain the differences between an element, compound, and mixture.

_____

_____

_____

_____

_____

9. A mixture is made by pouring sand in water. Some salt is added to the water, which is stirred until all the salt dissolves. Describe how you would separate the sand, salt, and water in this mixture.

_____

_____

_____

_____

_____

Lesson 1   Atoms and Elements

Write the letter of the word or words on the right in front of the appropriate definition or description on the left. You may use more than one letter from the right side to place in front of a number on the left side. A letter may be used more than once.

_____ 1. located in the nucleus of an atom	**a.** atom
_____ 2. column on a periodic table	**b.** neutrons
_____ 3. determines the order of the elements on a periodic table	**c.** oxygen
_____ 4. negatively charged particles	**d.** group
_____ 5. row on a periodic table	**e.** protons
_____ 6. move around the nucleus of an atom	**f.** atomic number
_____ 7. made by humans	**g.** electrons
_____ 8. positively charged particles	**h.** periodic table
_____ 9. organized arrangement of the elements	**i.** synthetic element
_____ 10. building block of matter	**j.** period
_____ 11. particles with no charge	
_____ 12. natural element	
_____ 13. smallest unit of an element that maintains the properties of that element	
_____ 14. particles that make up an atom	

Lesson 1   Compounds and Mixtures

Determine whether each of the following statements is true or false by circling the appropriate letter. If the statement is false, rewrite it so that it is true.

1. A mixture consists of two or more elements that are bonded to one another. T or F

_____

2. A compound contains elements in a fixed ratio. T or F

_____

3. Each component in a mixture maintains its own characteristics. T or F

_____

4. The properties of a compound are the same as the properties of the elements that make up the compound. T or F

_____

5. Water is a mixture made of hydrogen and oxygen. T or F

_____

6. The components of a mixture are easier to separate than the components of a compound. T or F

_____

7. A chemical formula can be used to represent a mixture. T or F

_____

8. Air is a compound that consists of several gases. T or F

_____

9. Compounds and mixtures can be either natural or synthetic. T or F

_____

Lesson 1   Pain Relievers

Read the following passage. Then answer the questions that follow the passage.

Aspirin is the most widely used drug in the world. The first use of aspirin can be traced back over 2000 years ago to the ancient Greeks and Romans. They discovered that the bark, fruit, and leaves from certain shrubs and trees were beneficial in treating a variety of ailments. They prepared extracts from different plants, especially the willow tree, to treat earaches, battle wounds, and eye diseases. Native Americans also used a bark extract to treat fever and pain.

In the early 1800s, German scientists isolated a compound called salicylic acid from the bark of willow trees. This compound was converted to another compound called sodium salicylate and sold to the public as a pain reliever. Unfortunately, sodium salicylate was found to be extremely irritating to the lining of the stomach. In the late 1800s, a German scientist named Felix Hoffmann discovered that salicylic acid could be converted to another compound called acetylsalicylic acid. This compound was not as irritating as sodium salicylate.

At the time, Hoffmann was working for the Bayer Company. In 1899, the company introduced acetylsalicylic acid to the public under the name Aspirin. If you check the label on a bottle of aspirin, you will see that the active ingredient is acetylsalicylic acid. The chemical formula for acetylsalicylic acid is $C_9H_8O_4$.

Salicylic acid, the compound originally used to relieve pain, is also used to make another compound called methyl salicylate. This compound is used in liniments that are applied to the body to relieve muscle aches and pains. This compound works by increasing the blood flow to the affected area and producing a feeling of warmth.

1. What are the four compounds mentioned in this passage that have been used as pain relievers?

_____

2. What three elements are present in the compound that is the active ingredient in aspirin?

_____

3. What two things do acetylsalicylic acid and methyl salicylate have in common?

_____

_____

4. Assume that an aspirin tablet is crushed and added to a glass of water. Has an element, compound, or mixture been prepared? Explain the reason for your choice.

_____

Lesson 1   Experiment: Separating the Components in a Mixture

You learned that the components in a mixture retain their properties and can be easily separated. In this experiment, you will separate the components in two different mixtures.

You Will Need

teaspoon   drinking glass
table salt   coffee filter
red pepper flakes   small pot
sheet of paper   stove (adult helper)
comb or glass rod   woolen cloth
sand

Procedure

1. Place a teaspoon of table salt and a teaspoon of red pepper on the paper. Mix the substances well.

2. Rub the comb or the glass rod with the woolen cloth. Rubbing with the woolen cloth produces electrical charges on the comb or rod.

3. Immediately bring the end of the comb or rod very close to, but not touching, the salt-pepper mixture on the paper.

4. Describe what happens to the mixture of salt and pepper flakes.

5. Discard the salt and pepper.

6. Place a teaspoon of table salt and a teaspoon of sand on the paper. Mix the substances well.

7. Place the mixture in a glass.

8. Pour water into the glass until it is half full. Stir the water.

9. Pour the mixture through the coffee filter. Collect the liquid that passes through the filter in the pot.

10. Describe what is trapped by the filter paper.

11. With adult supervision, carefully boil the liquid on the stove until all of the liquid has evaporated. Immediately remove the pot from the heat once all the liquid has evaporated.

12. Describe what remains in the pot after the liquid has completely evaporated.

Experiment: Separating the Components in a Mixture (cont'd.)

Results and Analysis

1. Which substance was attracted to the comb or rod? _____

2. Which substance was trapped on the coffee filter? _____

3. Which substance was left in the pot? _____

Conclusion

What conclusion can you draw based on your observations?

_____

_____

_____

_____

_____

_____

_____

_____

_____

_____

_____

_____

_____

_____

_____

_____

Lesson 2 Motions and Forces

If you have ever watched a baseball game on television, then you may have heard the announcer make comments such as these. "He threw that ball at 98 miles per hour." "That ball had a lot of spin on it." "Did you see how that ball dropped just as it reached the plate?" "That ball had a lot of movement on it." The announcer may not have known it, but he was talking about the baseball in terms of motions and forces. What you will learn in this lesson may help you impress your family and friends when you talk about a baseball in terms of its speed, velocity, acceleration, and momentum.

Motions and Forces

Whenever you see a baseball thrown by a pitcher, you know that the ball is moving. But did you know that you can tell if an object is moving only by looking at another object at the same time? For example, you may see the ball move across the field from the pitcher to the catcher. In this case, the ball moves, while the field stays in place. The object that stays in place is called a reference point. When an object changes position over time with respect to a reference point, the object is in **motion.**

The ball cannot be set in motion until a force acts on it. A **force** is simply a push or a pull. A pitcher provides the force on the ball by throwing it. Scientists express force using a unit called the **newton** (N). Usually, more than one force is acting on an object. As the ball travels to the catcher, another force is acting on it. This force is called air resistance. **Air resistance** is a force that opposes the motion of objects moving through the air.

No matter how many forces are acting on an object, an object may not move at all. Suppose two teams are competing in a tug-of-war contest. Each team is pulling on the rope in the opposite direction. What happens if each team applies the same amount of force? Assume that a team applies a force of 100 N in one direction. Also assume that the other team applies a force of 100 N in the opposite direction. In this case, the forces cancel each other. The net force on the rope is zero.

Key Terms

motion—the change in position of an object over time with respect to a reference point

force—a push or a pull

newton—the unit for force and weight

air resistance—the force that opposes the motion of objects moving through the air

net force—the combination of all the forces acting on an object

inertia—the tendency of an object to resist a change in motion

speed—the distance traveled by an object divided by the time it takes to travel that distance

velocity—the speed of an object in a particular direction

acceleration—the rate at which velocity changes

momentum—the quantity defined as the product of the mass and velocity of an object

law of conservation of momentum—the law that states that any time objects collide, the total amount of momentum stays the same

The **net force** is the combination of all the forces acting on an object.

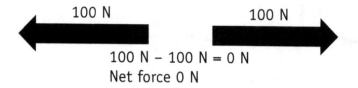

100 N $-$ 100 N = 0 N
Net force 0 N

Now assume that one team applies more force. One team may start to pull with a force of 120 N. If the other team continues to apply a force of 100 N, then the net force is 20 N. The rope will move in the direction of the net force.

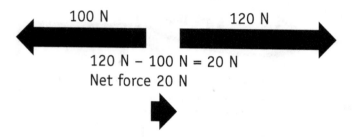

120 N $-$ 100 N = 20 N
Net force 20 N

Inertia

Objects have a natural tendency to resist a change in motion. If an object is at rest, the object will remain at rest until a force causes the object to move. Also, if an object is in motion, the object will keep on moving in the same direction and at the same speed until a force acts on it to change its direction or speed.

The tendency of an object to resist a change in motion is called **inertia**. Mass is a measure of inertia. The more mass an object has, the greater its inertia. A bowling ball has much more mass, and therefore more inertia, than a soccer ball. This is why it is much harder to get a bowling bowl moving. Once the bowling ball is moving, it will also be much harder to stop it than a moving soccer ball. Like all moving objects, both balls will have speed.

Speed

A pitcher may be able to throw a ball that reaches 95 miles per hour. This is the ball's speed. **Speed** is the distance traveled by an object divided by the time it takes to travel that distance. Obviously, the ball will not travel for 1 hour. But if it could, it would travel 95 miles in 1 hour at that speed. A radar gun is used to calculate the speed of the ball, just as a police officer uses a radar gun to determine the speed of a car. The radar gun gives the speed in miles per hour.

Speed can be expressed in various units in addition to miles per hour (mi/h). These units include feet per second (ft/s), and, in the metric system, meters per second (m/s) and kilometers per hour (km/h).

A radar gun determines the speed at a particular time. For example, a radar gun may show that a ball is moving at 20 miles per hour just after the pitcher has thrown it. The radar gun may show that a ball is moving at 95 miles per hour just before it reaches the batter. In any case, the ball does not move at the same speed from the time it is thrown by the pitcher until the time it reaches the batter. In other words, the ball does not move at a constant speed.

When the speed of an object is given, it is usually an average speed. The following equation is used to calculate the average speed.

$$\text{average speed} = \frac{\text{total distance}}{\text{total time}}$$

For example, if a car travels 400 miles in 8 hours, then its average speed is calculated as follows.

$$\text{average speed} = \frac{400 \text{ miles}}{8 \text{ hours}} = 50 \text{ miles/hour}$$

Speed can be plotted, as shown in the following graph.

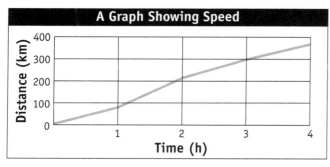

A Graph Showing Speed

Notice that the graph plots distance (km) versus time (h). The line on the graph is not a straight line because the speed changes. However, a total distance of 360 km has been traveled in a total time of 4 hours. Therefore, the average speed is (360 km)/(4 h) = 90 km/h.

Velocity

Suppose that two cars are traveling at 50 miles per hour on the same highway for 2 hours. Therefore, both cars travel 100 miles. However, the two cars do not wind up at the same place. In fact, they wind up 200 miles away from each other. How is this possible?

You may have figured out that the cars were traveling in opposite directions. Speed indicates distance and time but does not indicate anything about direction. If the direction is indicated, then you know an object's velocity. **Velocity** is the speed of an object in a particular direction.

Again suppose that two cars are traveling at 50 miles per hour along the same highway for 2 hours. However, this time you are told that the velocity of one car is 50 miles per hour west, and the velocity of the other car is 50 miles per hour east. If you know the cars' velocities, then it's no surprise that the cars wind up 200 miles away from each other. Notice that speed is indicated as 50 miles per hour, but velocity must include a direction—50 miles per hour west or 50 miles per hour east.

If the speed or the direction of an object changes, or both, then its velocity also changes.

For example, if a sailboat goes from 4 knots per hour to 7 knots per hour, then its velocity has changed. If the sailboat continues to move at 7 knots per hour but changes direction, then its velocity has again changed even though its speed remains constant.

Acceleration

Acceleration is the rate at which velocity changes. You learned that velocity changes if speed, direction, or both change. So an object accelerates if its speed, its direction, or both change. You can calculate the average acceleration of an object by using the following equation.

$$\text{average acceleration} = \frac{\text{final velocity minus starting velocity}}{\text{time it takes to change velocity}}$$

Like speed, acceleration can also be shown on a graph. In this case, acceleration is shown by plotting velocity versus time. Assume this graph plots the velocity of a car heading west.

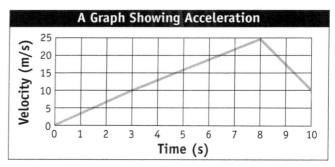

A Graph Showing Acceleration

Notice in the above graph that acceleration increases between 0 and 8 seconds and then decreases between 8 and 10 seconds. The increase in the graph represents *positive acceleration* when the velocity of the car is increasing. The decrease in the graph represents *negative acceleration* when the velocity of the car is decreasing. The faster the velocity changes, the greater the acceleration is.

The above graph shows that at 3 seconds, the velocity of the car was 10 m/s west. The velocity was 25 m/s west at 8 seconds. The average acceleration of the car between 3 and 8 seconds is calculated as follows.

$$\text{acceleration} = \frac{25 \text{ m/s} - 10 \text{ m/s}}{5 \text{ s}} = \frac{15 \text{ m/s}}{5 \text{ s}} = 3 \text{ m/s}^2$$

Momentum

You probably have heard a sports announcer say that the momentum has suddenly swung to the other team. The team with momentum may be getting hits, scoring goals, or making baskets.

You learned that a moving bowling ball has more inertia than a soccer ball and is therefore harder to stop. The bowling ball is also harder to stop because it has more momentum. The **momentum** of an object depends on its mass and the speed and direction in which it is traveling. Momentum can be calculated with the following equation.

momentum (p) = mass (m) × velocity (v)

A truck moving along a highway at 65 miles per hour has more momentum than a car traveling at 55 miles per hour for two reasons. First, the truck has more mass. Second, the truck is traveling faster. If both drivers apply their brakes, the truck will take longer to stop. Because it has more mass and therefore more inertia, the truck will also take longer to regain its momentum.

Law of Conservation of Momentum

When two moving objects collide, some or all of the momentum of one object is transferred to the other object. If only some of the momentum is transferred, then the rest of the momentum stays with the first object.

Consider what happens when a bowling ball hits the pins. As it rolls down the lane, the bowling ball has momentum. When it strikes the pins, some of this momentum is transferred to the pins it strikes. As a result, the pins move and fall over. Because it still has momentum, the bowling ball continues to move. Whatever momentum was lost by the bowling ball was gained by the pins that were hit.

Therefore, total momentum was neither gained nor lost. This is the **law of conservation of momentum**. This law states that any time objects collide, the total momentum stays the same.

Lesson 2   Review

Darken the circle by the best answer.

1. The tendency of an object in motion to remain in motion is known as the object's

   (A) inertia.

   (B) speed.

   (C) velocity.

   (D) acceleration.

2. What two factors must be known to calculate the speed of an object in motion?

   (A) direction and type of force being applied

   (B) distance and direction

   (C) distance and type of force being applied

   (D) distance and time

3. The law of conservation of momentum states that

   (A) momentum is lost in a collision.

   (B) when two objects collide, they will always bounce off each other.

   (C) when two objects collide, momentum may be transferred but is not lost.

   (D) if two objects stick together after a collision, then they both gain momentum.

4. Which of the following is not needed to determine the velocity of a moving truck?

   (A) its mass

   (B) the distance it travels

   (C) the time it takes to travel that distance

   (D) the direction in which it is traveling

5. What is the average acceleration of a train that speeds up from 9.6 m/s to 12 m/s in 0.8 s on a straight section of track?

   (A) 12 m/s^2 (C) 3 m/s^2

   (B) 9.6 m/s^2 (D) 2.4 m/s^2

6. How long will it take to drive a distance of 800 kilometers, if a car's average speed is 85 kilometers/hour? [Hint: Rearrange the formula for average speed to solve for time.]

   (A) 12.5 hours   (C) 8.5 hours

   (B) 9.4 hours   (D) 7.5 hours

7. Which of the following has the smallest amount of momentum?

   (A) a basketball player running down the court

   (B) a truck rolling down a highway

   (C) a child learning how to ride a bicycle

   (D) a jet plane being towed for takeoff

8. A car and a train are moving at the same velocity. However, they do not have the same momentum. How is this possible?

   _____

   _____

9. Explain why it is important for an airplane pilot to know wind velocity and not just the wind speed during a flight.

   _____

   _____

Lesson 2   Speed, Velocity, and Acceleration

In this lesson, you learned the difference between speed, velocity, and acceleration. Try to organize your knowledge by drawing a concept map. A concept map is begun by drawing a circle at the top of a piece of paper. The main idea is written in the center of this circle. The next step is to draw other circles beneath the first one you drew. Each of these circles contains an idea related to the main idea contained in the circle above. An arrow is then drawn from the main circle to each of the circles below. One or a few words are written near each arrow to show the relation between the circles. If needed, more circles and arrows are drawn beneath the first set of circles.

   Use the following terms to create a concept map: speed, velocity, acceleration, force, direction, and motion. There is more than one way to draw a concept map. The following is just a suggestion to get started.

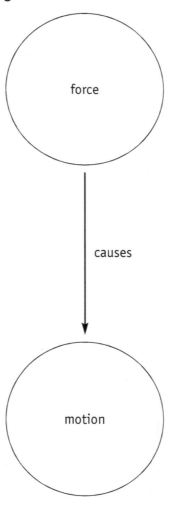

Lesson 2 — Motions and Forces Crossword Puzzle

Across

2. factor that affects an object's momentum
6. unit for force
8. combination of all the forces acting on an object (two words)
9. tendency for an object at rest to remain at rest
10. distance traveled divided by the time taken
11. mass times velocity

Down

1. a push or pull
3. change in velocity over time
4. what happens to momentum when moving objects collide
5. what you need to know to indicate an object's velocity
7. speed in a particular direction
10. a word that might be used to describe velocity

Lesson 2   Problem Solving

Use what you learned in this lesson to solve the following problems dealing with the motion of objects.

1. What is the net force on the following object? In which direction will the object move?

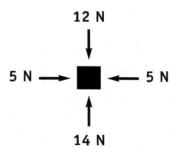

2. An airplane flies from San Francisco to Chicago, a distance of 1260 km, in 3.5 hours. What is the average speed of this plane?

3. Does the following graph show positive acceleration or negative acceleration? Explain the reason for your choice.

4. Jorge has a mass of 45 kilograms and is skateboarding with a velocity of 3 meters/second north. What is Jorge's momentum? The units for momentum are kg•m/s north.

5. Calculate the acceleration of the object from the data listed in the following table.

Time (seconds)	Velocity (meters per second east)
0	0
1	5
2	10
3	15
4	20

Lesson 2   Experiment: Comparing Momentums

You learned that the momentum of an object is determined by multiplying its velocity times its mass. An object that is not moving has no velocity and therefore no momentum. From the equation for calculating momentum, you can also tell that the more mass or greater velocity an object has, the more momentum it has. In this experiment, you will explore the relationship between mass, velocity, and momentum.

You Will Need

two books
ruler with groove
scissors
paper or plastic cup
four marbles
measuring tape

Procedure

1. Place one of the books on the floor.

2. Set one end of the ruler on the book to make a ramp that is at least 2 inches high.

3. Cut a section from the lip of the cup large enough for a marble to pass through the opening.

4. Place the cup upside down on the floor so that the opening is against the ruler.

5. Place a marble in the groove of the ruler at the top of the ramp.

6. Release the marble so that it enters the cup.

7. Measure the distance the cup moved along the floor.

8. Repeat steps 4–7 four more times and average your results.

9. Repeat steps 4–7 four more times using two marbles and average your results.

10. Repeat steps 4–7 four more times using three marbles and average your results.

11. Repeat steps 4–7 four more times using four marbles and average your results.

12. Place a second book on top of the first book and repeat steps 4–11.

Experiment: Comparing Momentums (cont'd.)

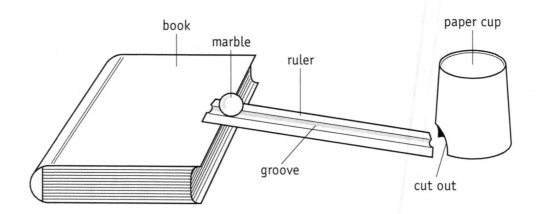

book   marble   ruler   paper cup   groove   cut out

Results and Analysis

1. Organize your data into a table.

	One marble	Two marbles	Three marbles	Four marbles
One book				
Trial 1				
Trial 2				
Trial 3				
Trial 4				
Trial 5				
Average				
Two Books				
Trial 1				
Trial 2				
Trial 3				
Trial 4				
Trial 5				
Average				

Experiment: Comparing Momentums (cont'd.)

2. How are you affecting momentum by using more marbles?

_____

_____

3. How are you affecting momentum by using two books?

_____

_____

Conclusion

What conclusion can you draw based on your results?

_____

_____

_____

_____

_____

_____

_____

_____

_____

_____

_____

_____

_____

_____

Lesson 3 Transfer of Energy

Look around you. What do you see? Perhaps you see members of your family, a pet, or trees outside a window. Whatever you see is visible only if there is light present. If it were totally dark, you would not be able to see any of these things. The light that makes it possible to see things may come from the sun or a lamp. No matter where it comes from, light is a form of energy. In this lesson, you will learn more about energy and light.

Energy and Light

If you ask ten people what energy is, you are likely to get ten different answers. In science, however, energy has just one meaning. **Energy** is the ability to do work. You use energy to turn the pages of a book, a radio uses energy to make sounds, and a solar-powered calculator uses energy to function. There are different forms of energy. You depend on chemical energy to turn the pages. A radio uses electrical energy to make sounds. A calculator uses light energy to function.

Light is a form of energy that travels as a wave. Sound is also a form of energy that travels as a wave. Sound waves travel through the air, which is a type of matter. Light waves can also travel through the air and other forms of matter. However, light

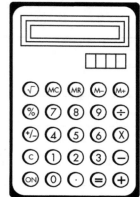

waves can also travel through empty space. Sunlight must first pass through empty space before it reaches Earth.

Electromagnetic Waves

Light energy travels as an electromagnetic wave. An **electromagnetic wave** is a wave that can travel through empty space or matter. As its name suggests, an electromagnetic wave consists of both electric and magnetic fields.

Key Terms

energy—the ability to do work

electromagnetic wave—a wave that can travel through empty space or matter

radiation—the transfer of energy as electromagnetic waves

wavelength—the distance from any point on a wave to the next corresponding point on the wave

scattering—the change in the direction of light waves that collide and bounce off particles

reflection—the bouncing of light waves off the surface of an object

refraction—the bending of light as it passes from one type of matter to another

absorption—the process that occurs when the energy carried by light waves is transferred to the particles of matter

global warming—the warming of Earth caused by the atmosphere's trapping of light waves from the sun

An electric field is a force that exists around every object that has a charge. Suppose you rub two balloons with a wool cloth. Rubbing the balloons causes each one to have a charge. Because they have the same charge, the balloons will repel each other when they are brought together. If you hold one balloon near the wool cloth, they will attract each other because they have opposite charges.

A magnetic field is a force that exists around every magnet. Because of its magnetic field, a magnet attracts metallic objects such as paper clips and thumbtacks.

Radiation

Particles vibrate or move quickly back and forth. When a particle with a charge vibrates, the electric field surrounding this particle also vibrates. The vibrating electric field then creates a vibrating magnetic field. Together, the vibrating electric and magnetic fields create an electromagnetic wave. The following sequence shows how an electromagnetic wave is created.

vibrating charged particle

↓

vibrating electric field

↓

**vibrating magnetic field
(plus the vibrating electric field)**

↓

electromagnetic wave

The energy of the vibrating particle has been transferred to the electromagnetic wave. The electromagnetic wave can then carry the energy and transfer it to other objects. The transfer of energy as electromagnetic waves is called **radiation**.

Visible Light

The electromagnetic waves from the sun are the major source of energy on Earth. This is surprising when you consider that only a very small amount of the total energy given off by the sun reaches Earth. Most of the sun's energy travels out through space toward other parts of the universe.

The electromagnetic waves from the sun travel at 186,000 miles per second or about 700,000,000 miles per hour. This is about 880,000 times faster than the speed of sound waves. Despite their incredible speed, electromagnetic waves from the sun still take about 8 minutes to reach Earth. They take this long because the sun is over 90 million miles from Earth.

The light we see is only a fraction of all the electromagnetic waves that come from the sun. Those waves that we do see make up visible light. The visible light from the sun is white light. White light consists of all colors of light, ranging from red to violet. These are the colors that you see in a rainbow when water droplets separate white light into its various colors.

Lesson 3, Transfer of Energy
Science 7, SV 9781419034350

Each color of light has a different wavelength. A **wavelength** is the distance from any point on a wave to the next corresponding point on the wave. Violet light has a shorter wavelength than red light. The shorter the wavelength, the more energy it has. Therefore, violet light has more energy than red light.

Wave

Wavelength

Wavelength

Invisible Light

Most electromagnetic waves are not visible. Arranged from longer to shorter wavelengths, these waves include radio waves, microwaves, infrared waves, ultraviolet rays, X-rays, and gamma rays. Both radios and televisions broadcast radio waves. Microwaves are used in ovens, cell phones, and radar devices. Infrared lamps give off heat to keep foods warm.

Ultraviolet rays can be a health hazard. Overexposure to these waves can cause skin damage and cancer. However, ultraviolet rays can also be a health benefit. These rays help the body produce vitamin D, which is needed for healthy teeth and bones.

X-rays are used in medicine to see inside a person's body and in security devices to see inside bags and other containers. Gamma rays are used to treat some forms of cancer and to kill harmful bacteria in foods. So, even though you cannot see these electromagnetic waves, they can be very useful.

Scattering of Light

Electromagnetic waves behave in various ways when they strike an object. How light behaves depends on the nature of the object. To understand what happens when electromagnetic waves strike an object, let's consider visible light simply because we can see it.

Have you ever noticed that the light from a flashlight gets dimmer as it travels through the air?

The light gets dimmer in part because of scattering. **Scattering** occurs when light waves change direction as they collide and bounce off the particles in air. After they bounce off the particles, the light waves scatter in different directions. As the waves scatter, the light gets dimmer.

The scattering of light can produce a reflection. A **reflection** occurs when light waves bounce off an object. Light bounces off both a mirror and a wall. However, you can see your reflection only in a mirror. The reason has to do with the differences in the surfaces of a mirror and a wall. The surface of a mirror is very smooth. When light strikes a mirror, all the waves are reflected at the same angle. All these reflected light waves reach your eyes. Therefore, you can see them.

The surface of a wall is not as smooth. When light strikes a wall, the waves are reflected at many different angles. Most of the reflected waves do not reach your eyes. Therefore, you cannot see any reflection from a wall when light strikes it.

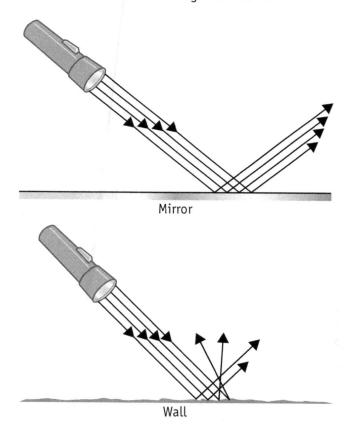

Mirror

Wall

Transmission of Light

Sometimes light does not bounce off an object. Instead, it is transmitted through an object. In other words, light passes through the surface and into the substance or object. For example, light can pass through the water. As light passes from the air into the water, it bends. The bending of light as it passes from one type of matter to another is known as **refraction**. Refraction occurs because the speed of light waves depends on the material through which the waves are traveling. Light waves travel at different speeds in air and water.

This difference in speeds produces an optical illusion. When you look at an object underwater, the light waves reflecting off the surface of the object do not travel to your eyes in a straight path. Rather, they are bent or refracted. As a result, the object you see underwater is not actually in the spot where you think it is. Refraction makes it seem as if the object is in the spot where you are looking.

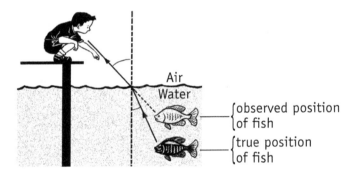

Absorption of Light

You can see some objects, such as the sun, because they emit light. You can see other objects, such as this page, because they reflect light. However, you cannot see an object if it absorbs all the light that strikes it. **Absorption** occurs when the energy carried by light waves is transferred to the particles of matter. Because the particles of matter absorb the energy, then no light is reflected. If no light is reflected, then the object is not visible.

The particles in a dark object absorb light waves better than the particles in a lighter object. Dark color clothes absorb light waves better than light color clothes. When there is little light during the night, the dark color clothes absorb almost all the light. This is why it is difficult to see a person wearing dark clothes at night.

Global Warming

The gases in the air, such as oxygen and carbon dioxide, make up Earth's atmosphere. The atmosphere acts like the windows on a greenhouse. Light waves from the sun pass through the atmosphere and strike Earth. Some of these waves are absorbed. Others are reflected back up into the atmosphere. Some of the waves reflected into the atmosphere pass back into space. Others, however, are reflected back down to Earth. As a result, some of the light waves are trapped by the atmosphere and are prevented from escaping back into space.

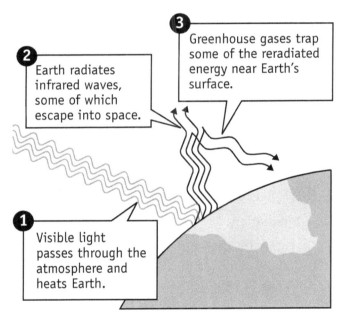

Just like a greenhouse, Earth is warmed by the energy carried by the light waves trapped by the atmosphere. This process is known as **global warming**. Scientists are not sure how much warmer Earth will get. However, even a slight increase in Earth's average temperature can have disastrous consequences. For example, glaciers can melt, causing a rise in sea levels. In turn, communities and homes along a coastline can flood. Global warming can also cause droughts that will affect all areas.

Lesson 3

Review

Darken the circle by the best answer.

1. You can see the moon at night because it
   - Ⓐ absorbs light.
   - Ⓑ reflects light.
   - Ⓒ transmits light.
   - Ⓓ refracts light.

2. Which of the following electromagnetic waves have the highest energy?
   - Ⓐ radio waves
   - Ⓑ infrared waves
   - Ⓒ visible light
   - Ⓓ X-rays

3. The transfer of energy as electromagnetic waves is known as
   - Ⓐ refraction.
   - Ⓑ reflection.
   - Ⓒ radiation.
   - Ⓓ global warming.

4. A vibrating charged particle creates
   - Ⓐ a vibrating magnetic field.
   - Ⓑ a vibrating electric field.
   - Ⓒ electromagnetic waves.
   - Ⓓ All of the above

5. The scattering of light occurs when particles
   - Ⓐ cause light to change direction.
   - Ⓑ absorb light.
   - Ⓒ stop vibrating.
   - Ⓓ change the wavelength of light.

6. Infrared light is used to
   - Ⓐ produce sounds.
   - Ⓑ keep foods warm.
   - Ⓒ synthesize vitamin D.
   - Ⓓ treat certain types of cancers.

7. Which of the following statements is true?
   - Ⓐ All electromagnetic waves are visible.
   - Ⓑ The longer the wavelength of light, the more energy it has.
   - Ⓒ Ultraviolet rays can be beneficial.
   - Ⓓ Darker colors absorb fewer light waves compared to lighter colors.

8. How do sunshades set up in the windshields of cars help keep the interior cool?

   _____

   _____

   _____

   _____

9. Describe three ways in which electromagnetic waves have been useful to you today.

   _____

   _____

   _____

   _____

   _____

Lesson 3

Glowing Meat

Read the following passage and then answer the questions.

In 2005, a man in Australia called a local radio station to see if any listeners could help him with a strange problem. The man reported that when he opened the door to his refrigerator, the pork chops inside were glowing. He was wondering if anyone knew why the meat was glowing and if the pork chops were safe to eat.

The story reached scientists working in a government agency concerned with food safety. They reported that the glowing pork contained bacteria that emit light. You may have seen fireflies that emit light. The bacteria that emit light are called *Pseudomonas fluorescens*. The second part of their name comes from the word *fluorescent*. You probably have seen a fluorescent light, possibly at school or in your home.

A fluorescent light contains gas under low pressure. When electricity passes through this gas, it emits ultraviolet light. Recall that ultraviolet light is invisible. So how does a fluorescent bulb emit visible light? The inside of a fluorescent bulb is coated with a substance called phosphor. Phosphors absorb ultraviolet light and in turn emit visible light. The color of this visible light depends on what kinds of phosphors are used to coat the bulb.

By the way, the scientists told the man that *Pseudomonas fluorescen*s is not known to cause food poisoning. However, they told the man to throw away the meat because these bacteria grow quickly on meat that is starting to spoil. Therefore, the meat likely contained bacteria that do cause food poisoning. So it's not a good idea to eat glowing meat.

1. What do fireflies and *Pseudomonas fluorescens* have in common?

_____

2. Suppose a fluorescent light bulb was not coated with phosphors. How would this affect the light it produces?

_____

_____

3. Why would a fluorescent light bulb that has not been coated with phosphors be dangerous to a person's health?

_____

_____

4. If *Pseudomonas fluorescens* does not cause food poisoning, then why did the scientists tell the man to throw the glowing meat into the garbage?

_____

Lesson 3

The Speed of Light

In Lesson 2, you learned how to calculate speed by using the following equation.

$$\text{average speed} = \frac{\text{total distance}}{\text{total time}}$$

Use the above equation to solve the following problems. Recall that the speed of light is 186,000 miles per second. You may have to rearrange the above equation to answer a problem.

1. How long does it take for sunlight to reach Mercury, which is 34,175,000 miles away?

2. We see the moon because light from the sun reflects from the moon's surface. How long does it take for this reflected light to reach Earth? The moon is about 240,000 miles from Earth.

3. Light takes about 43 minutes to travel from the sun to Jupiter. How far away is Jupiter from the sun? Hint: Be sure to change the time in minutes into seconds.

4. If light travels 880,000 times faster than the speed of sound, what is the speed of sound?

Lesson 3   Reflection, Refraction, and Absorption

Explain how either reflection, refraction, or absorption of light is involved in each of the following situations.

1. Birds such as terns fly above the water and search for food. When a bird spots a fish, the bird quickly dives underwater to catch it. What must the bird do when it dives underwater?

   _____

   _____

   _____

2. You check the time by looking at a clock in the mirror. The time appears to be 9 o'clock, but it is actually 3 o'clock.

   _____

   _____

   _____

3. You wake up at 3 o'clock in the morning and decide to get something to drink. You bump into a dark wall on your way to the kitchen.

   _____

   _____

   _____

4. Plants look green because they absorb all the visible colors except green light. What do plants do with the green light that strikes them? What color would a plant be if it is placed in red light? Why?

   _____

   _____

   _____

   _____

   _____

Lesson 3   Experiment: Pouring Light

You learned that light is refracted as it passes from the air into water. In this experiment, you will see how light can also be reflected in water.

You Will Need

hammer
nail
glass jar with a screw-on lid
newspaper
masking tape
flashlight
bucket
dark closet

Procedure

1. Use the hammer and nail to poke two holes across from each other through the lid of the jar.

2. Fill the jar three-quarters full with water.

3. Wrap several layers of newspaper around the jar.

4. Use masking tape to keep the newspaper wrapped snugly against the jar.

5. Take the flashlight, jar, and small bucket into the closet.

6. Turn on the flashlight and close the closet door.

7. Hold the jar on top of the flashlight.

8. Slowly pour the water from the jar into the bucket.

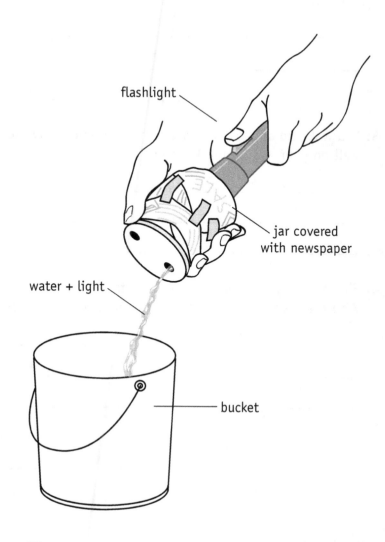

flashlight

jar covered with newspaper

water + light

bucket

Experiment: Pouring Light (cont'd.)

Results and Analysis

1. Describe what you see as the water flows from the jar.

_____

_____

_____

_____

_____

_____

2. Explain why the light travels through the water and not out the jar.

_____

_____

_____

_____

_____

Conclusion

What conclusion can you draw from your observation?

_____

_____

_____

_____

_____

Lesson 4 Structure and Function in Living Systems

All living things, or **organisms**, are made of cells. A **cell** is the smallest unit of an organism that can perform all life processes. Similar cells work together to form a **tissue**. For example, muscle cells make up muscle tissue. Two or more tissues work together to form an **organ**. For example, muscle tissue and nervous tissue make up the stomach. Organs that work together make up an **organ system**.

Key Terms

organism—a living thing

cell—the smallest unit of an organism that can perform all life processes

tissue—a group of cells that work together for a specific job

organ—a group of tissues that work together for a specific job

organ system—a group of organs that work together for a specific job

joint—the place where two bones meet

ligament—the tissue that connects two bones at a joint

cartilage—the soft tissue that prevents bones from rubbing against each other

skeletal muscle—a voluntary muscle that is responsible for moving a part of the body

tendon—the tissue that connects a muscle to a bone

smooth muscle—an involuntary muscle found in internal organs

cardiac muscle—the type of muscle that makes up the walls of the heart

esophagus—a muscular tube that connects the mouth to the stomach

pharynx—a passageway for both food and air

trachea—a passageway that connects the pharynx to the lungs

larynx—the voice box

epiglottis—a tiny flap that covers the trachea

bronchus—one of the two branches of the trachea that leads to the lungs

alveolus—a tiny air sac in the lungs

diaphragm—the muscle that controls breathing

atrium—an upper chamber of the heart

ventricle—a lower chamber of the heart

vein—a vessel that returns blood from all parts of the body to the heart

artery—a vessel that carries blood from the heart to all parts of the body

capillary—a blood vessel through which substances such as oxygen can pass

hemoglobin—a substance that carries oxygen in the red blood cells

The stomach works with other organs to make up the digestive system. Organisms, such as humans, contain several organ systems that all work together to carry out life processes and maintain good health.

The Skeletal and Muscular Systems

An adult human body contains slightly more than 200 bones. These bones form the skeleton. This skeleton serves several functions: (1) supports the body, (2) protects internal organs such as the heart, (3) stores minerals such as calcium, and (4) works with muscles so that the body can move. In addition, some bones produce blood cells.

The place where two bones meet is known as a **joint**. The two bones are held together at a joint by a **ligament**. The parts of the bones that come in contact with each other at a joint are covered with a softer material called **cartilage**. This cartilage prevents any wearing away of bones caused by rubbing against each other. However, the cartilage can become thinner, leading to a disease called arthritis. When this happens, the bones rub against each other, causing pain. Another bone disease is osteoporosis by which the bones become weak and break more easily.

Muscles make up about one-third the mass of the body. There are three kinds of muscles. **Skeletal muscles** are responsible for moving parts of the body, such as the arms and legs. Skeletal muscles are connected to a bone by a **tendon**. Because their actions can be deliberately controlled, skeletal muscles are known as voluntary muscles. Voluntary muscles usually work in pairs. One muscle is called a *flexor* because it bends a body part, such as an arm. The other muscle is called an *extensor* because it straightens out the body part.

A second kind of muscle is smooth muscle. **Smooth muscles** are found in the walls of the stomach, blood vessels, and other internal organs. Because their actions cannot be deliberately controlled, smooth muscles are known as involuntary muscles.

The third type of muscle is **cardiac muscle**, which makes up the walls of the heart. Cardiac muscle is unique in that it can beat in a rhythmic pattern. Cardiac muscle can be damaged by a heart attack.

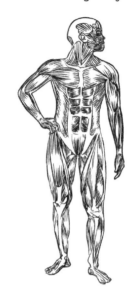

The Digestive System

The digestive system breaks down foods into substances that cells can use. This system consists of a tube that begins at the mouth and ends at the anus. Between the mouth and the anus are several organs that aid in digestion.

Digestion begins in the mouth. Teeth physically break down food. Chemicals in saliva begin to break down starches. The food then passes through the **esophagus** and enters the stomach. Digestion continues in the stomach as proteins are broken down. Next the food passes into the small intestine. Digestion is completed in the small intestine. The digestion of fats involves a substance made by the liver. This substance is called bile. Bile breaks down fats into smaller droplets, making it easier to digest them. The digested materials are absorbed by the small intestine. Undigested material passes into the large intestine where it remains until it is eliminated through the anus.

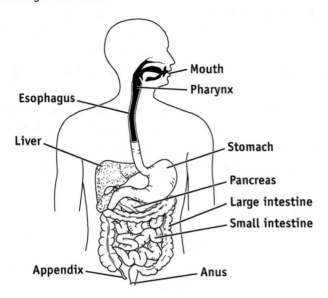

The Respiratory System

The function of the respiratory system is to get oxygen to the cells and remove the carbon dioxide they produce. Air enters the body through the nasal passages or the mouth where it is filtered and moistened. The air then passes into the **pharynx**, which is the throat. The pharynx branches into two tubes. One is the esophagus. The other branch is the **trachea**, or windpipe. The upper end of the trachea contains the **larynx**, or voice box.

When food is swallowed, a tiny flap called the **epiglottis** presses down and shuts the opening to the trachea. This prevents a person from choking on food. When air is taken in, the epiglottis is in the upright position. This allows air to enter the trachea.

The trachea branches into two **bronchi.** Each bronchus leads to a lung. The bronchi branch into smaller and smaller tubes. Eventually, the air reaches an **alveolus**, or tiny air sac. Each lung contains nearly 300 million alveoli. In each alveolus, oxygen from the air enters the body. Carbon dioxide from the body

enters the alveolus. From here, the carbon dioxide will follow the same route, but in reverse order, that oxygen took on its journey through the respiratory system.

Breathing is controlled by a muscle called the **diaphragm.** The diaphragm contracts and moves downward to increase the volume or space inside the chest cavity. This decreases the pressure inside the chest cavity. As a result, air from the outside moves into the nasal passages and begins traveling through the respiratory system. The diaphragm then relaxes, forcing air out of the lungs.

Disorders involving the respiratory system affect millions of people. These disorders include asthma, which develops when the passages to the alveoli get too narrow for air to pass through. Another disorder is emphysema, in which the alveoli are damaged. As a result, people with emphysema have trouble getting enough oxygen.

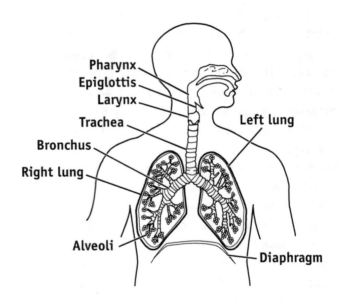

The Circulatory System

The heart is the main organ of the circulatory system. The heart's only function is to pump blood throughout the body. Use the following illustration of the heart to see how blood flows through the body.

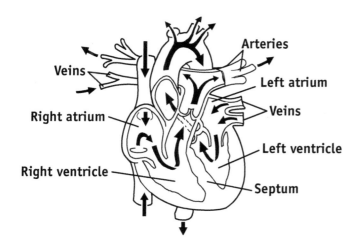

Veins — **Arteries**

Left atrium

Veins

Right atrium

Left ventricle

Right ventricle — **Septum**

A wall called the septum divides the heart into right and left sides. Each side is further divided into an upper and lower chamber. An upper chamber is called an **atrium**. A lower chamber is called a **ventricle**. The right side of the heart pumps blood to the lungs. Blood returns from the lungs and enters the left side of the heart. The left side of the heart then pumps blood to all parts of the body except the lungs. Valves keep the blood flowing in one direction.

Blood returns to the heart from parts of the body through vessels called **veins**. Blood flowing through veins contains a high concentration of carbon dioxide and a low concentration of oxygen. This blood enters the right atrium and then passes to the right ventricle where it is pumped to the lungs. Blood leaving the heart travels through vessels called **arteries**.

At the lungs, the blood vessels branch into tiny vessels called **capillaries**. Oxygen and carbon dioxide are exchanged between a capillary and an alveolus. Blood that has a high concentration of oxygen then returns to the left atrium and passes into the left ventricle before it travels to various parts of the body.

Oxygen is carried by the red blood cells. These cells contain a substance called **hemoglobin** that carries the oxygen. The blood also contains white blood cells that help protect against diseases. Tiny particles called platelets are also found in the blood. Platelets are needed for blood to clot. Blood cannot clot without medication in a person with a disease called hemophilia. An injury may result in internal bleeding that cannot be stopped without emergency treatment.

Lesson 4, Structure and Function in Living Systems
Science 7, SV 9781419034350

Lesson 4

Review

Darken the circle for the best answer.

1. A muscle is connected to a bone by a(n)
   - Ⓐ joint.
   - Ⓒ tendon.
   - Ⓑ ligament.
   - Ⓓ epiglottis.

2. Blood returning from the lungs enters the
   - Ⓐ right atrium.
   - Ⓒ left atrium.
   - Ⓑ right ventricle.
   - Ⓓ left ventricle.

3. Where does the process of digestion <u>not</u> occur?
   - Ⓐ esophagus
   - Ⓒ stomach
   - Ⓑ mouth
   - Ⓓ small intestine

4. The tiny air sacs in the lungs are called
   - Ⓐ bronchi.
   - Ⓒ atria.
   - Ⓑ capillaries.
   - Ⓓ alveoli.

5. Which of the following statements is true?
   - Ⓐ The respiratory system transports oxygen to parts of the body.
   - Ⓑ The digestive system is made partly of cardiac muscle.
   - Ⓒ The circulatory system allows blood to flow in only one direction.
   - Ⓓ The skeletal system is made completely from cartilage.

6. Which is a disease that affects the respiratory system?
   - Ⓐ arthritis
   - Ⓒ hemophilia
   - Ⓑ emphysema
   - Ⓓ tendonitis

7. Which system makes up about one-third of the mass of the human body?
   - Ⓐ circulatory system
   - Ⓑ digestive system
   - Ⓒ muscular system
   - Ⓓ skeletal system

8. How is food prevented from passing into the trachea when swallowing so that a person does not choke?

   _____

   _____

   _____

9. A capillary is only one cell thick. How is the structure of a capillary related to its function?

   _____

   _____

   _____

Lesson 4

Ulcers

Read the following passage and then answer the questions.

An ulcer is a sore that develops in the digestive system. This sore can develop in the lining of the stomach or in the upper part of the small intestine called the duodenum. This sore is called a peptic ulcer. These ulcers can be quite painful and can cause internal bleeding. In many cases, an operation must be performed to remove the affected area of the digestive system.

For almost 100 years, people believed that stress, spicy foods, and alcohol caused most ulcers. Even doctors thought so. Then in 1982, two doctors discovered that most ulcers are caused by bacteria that grow in the stomach. The scientific name for these bacteria is *Helicobacter pylori*, known simply as *H. pylori*. About 20 percent of people under 40 and more than 50 percent of those over 60 have these bacteria in their digestive systems. Scientists are not sure how people become infected with *H. pylori* bacteria. But strangely enough, most people infected with *H. pylori* don't develop an ulcer.

Doctors aren't completely sure why, but they think that part of the reason may depend on the individual person. People who develop ulcers may already have a problem with the lining of their stomachs. For example, such people may naturally secrete more stomach acid than others, and it doesn't matter what stresses they're exposed to or what foods they eat.

When *H. pylori* bacteria do cause ulcers, here's how doctors think these ulcers develop:

(1) bacteria weaken the protective coating of the stomach and upper small intestine,

(2) acid in the stomach then gets through to the sensitive tissues lining the digestive system underneath, and

(3) acid and bacteria directly irritate this lining, resulting in sores, or ulcers.

Although *H. pylori* are responsible for most cases of peptic ulcers, these ulcers can happen for other reasons, too. Sometimes people regularly take pain relievers (like aspirin or ibuprofen) that fight inflammation in the body. These medications, known as nonsteroidal anti-inflammatory drugs (NSAIDs), are used to treat certain long-term painful conditions like arthritis. If taken in high daily doses over a long period of time, they can cause ulcers in some of the people who use them. Smoking can also cause ulcers. What about stress, spicy foods, and alcohol? These may not cause ulcers, but they can make them worse.

1. What are three causes of peptic ulcers?

_____

_____

_____

2. Why doesn't everyone infected with *H. pylori* develop ulcers?

_____

_____

_____

3. Why are antibiotics used to treat ulcers?

_____

_____

_____

Lesson 4

The Circulatory System

The following illustration shows how blood flows through the heart. Keep in mind that the right side of the heart is on the left as you look at this illustration. It's as if this heart is in a person who is facing you.

1. Where is blood heading after it leaves structure 3?

_____

_____

2. Where is blood heading after it leaves structure 5?

_____

_____

3. What is the name of structure 1?

_____

4. Which structures represent arteries?

_____

5. What is the function of structure 4?

_____

6. Why do the arrows point in only one direction?

_____

7. Which structures contain blood that has a high concentration of oxygen?

_____

Lesson 4

Experiment: The Digestive System

Digestion changes foods to produce new substances that cells can use. The changes that occur during digestion are known as chemical changes or chemical reactions. During digestion, chemical reactions occur in the mouth, stomach, and small intestine. These chemical reactions occur faster with the help of an enzyme. An enzyme is a chemical substance that speeds up the rate of a reaction. In the following experiment, you will examine how an enzyme can speed up digestion.

You Will Need

gelatin dessert
knife
ruler
five clear drinking glasses
masking tape
marker
teaspoon
meat tenderizer
measuring cup
pineapple juice
apple juice
orange juice
water

Procedure

1. Prepare the gelatin dessert according to the directions on the package. Refrigerate until it is a solid.

2. Cut five 1-inch square pieces of solid gelatin.

3. Place each piece in a separate glass. Labels the glasses A, B, C, D, and E.

4. Dissolve 1 teaspoon of meat tenderizer in 4 ounces of water.

Experiment: The Digestive System (cont'd.)

5. Add one of the following to each of the glasses:

   a. 4 ounces of water

   b. 4 ounces of the meat tenderizer solution

   c. 4 ounces of pineapple juice

   d. 4 ounces of apple juice

   e. 4 ounces of orange juice

6. Allow the gelatin pieces to soak at room temperature for 24 hours.

Results and Analysis

1. Describe the appearance of the gelatin cube in each glass.

   _____

   _____

   _____

2. As the gelatin is digested, the cube gets smaller. Which solutions digest the gelatin?

   _____

3. What do all the solutions in the answer to question 2 contain?

   _____

Conclusion

What conclusion can you draw based on your results?

   _____

   _____

Lesson 5 Reproduction and Heredity

In the middle 1800s, an Austrian monk named Gregor Mendel studied pea plants. He was interested in learning how traits are passed from parents to offspring. People had long recognized that this was part of reproduction. But no one could establish how it happened—until Mendel discovered the answer.

Genetics and Heredity

The field of biology that investigates how traits are transmitted from parents to offspring is called **genetics**. Mendel's work with pea plants formed the basis of genetics. His results explained how heredity operates. **Heredity** is the passing of traits from parents to offspring. Mendel studied seven traits in pea plants. Each trait occurs in two contrasting forms, as shown in the following table.

Plant height	Tall stem	Short stem
Pod color	Green	Yellow
Pod appearance	Inflated	Constricted
Seed texture	Smooth	Wrinkled
Seed color	Yellow	Green
Flower position on stem	Axial (along stem)	Terminal (at tip)
Flower color	Purple	White

Key Terms

genetics—the field of science that investigates how traits are passed from parents to offspring

heredity—the passing of traits from parents to offspring

dominant trait—a trait that appears in the first generation of parents that have different traits

recessive trait—a trait that does not appear in the first generation of parents that have different traits

gene—a segment of a chromosome that determines a particular trait

allele—the different forms of the same gene

Punnett square—a grid to organize all the possible combinations of offspring

homozygous—the situation where both alleles for a gene are identical

heterozygous—the situation where the two alleles for a gene are different

phenotype—the appearance of an organism

genotype—the genetic makeup of an organism

testcross—a genetic cross used to determine the genotype of an organism

Mendel collected the seeds from his pea plants. He planted the seeds the following year and observed which traits appeared. At first, Mendel's observations confused him. For example, he observed that the seeds from tall plants grew into both tall plants and short plants. He also observed that the seeds from purple-flowering plants grew into plants with purple flowers and plants with white flowers. Mendel set about to find out what was happening.

Mendel studied each trait and its contrasting forms individually. He controlled how the plants reproduced. In other words, he eliminated any possibility that birds, insects, or the wind could carry pollen from one plant to another plant. Mendel began by developing plants that were pure for each trait.

He developed plants that were pure for long stems and plants that were pure for short stems. All these tall plants and short plants were identical for the other six characteristics, such as pod color and seed texture. Mendel eventually obtained 14 lines of pure plants, one for each of the 14 contrasting traits.

Once Mendel was satisfied that his plants were pure for a particular trait, he performed a cross by taking the pollen from one type of plant and placing it on another type of plant. For example, Mendel took the pollen from a plant that was pure for tall stem and dusted it on a plant that was pure for short stem. He did this for all seven traits. All the plants in these crosses are known as parental plants. Mendel labeled each of these parental plants as belonging to the P_1 generation. Plants produced by crossing the P_1 generation are known as the F_1 generation.

Dominant and Recessive Traits

Mendel noticed that all the plants in the F_1 generation displayed only one of the traits present in the P_1 generation. For example, in crosses between plants with tall stems and plants with short stems, all the plants in the F_1 generation had tall stems. Crossing plants with yellow seed color and plants with green seed color produced F_1 plants that all had yellow seed color.

Mendel concluded that one trait for each characteristic prevented the other trait from having any effect. Mendel suggested that the trait appearing in the F_1 generation was controlled by a dominant factor because it overshadowed, or dominated, the other factor. For example, Mendel called tall stem a **dominant trait**. The trait that did not appear in the F_1 generation was controlled by a recessive factor. Mendel called short stem a **recessive trait**. Mendel determined which traits in pea plants were dominant and which traits were recessive.

Dominant trait	Recessive trait
Tall stem	Short stem
Green pod	Yellow pod
Inflated pod	Constricted pod
Smooth seed	Wrinkled seed
Yellow seed	Green seed
Axial flower	Terminal flower
Purple flower	White flower

Genes and Alleles

Mendel used the term *factor* to describe what controls a trait. Today, scientists use the term *gene*. A **gene** is a segment of a chromosome that determines a particular trait. A chromosome is the structure in a cell that stores the hereditary information. A gene can have different forms. Different forms of the same gene are called **alleles**. Each cell usually has two alleles for each trait. However, the reproductive cells have only one allele for each trait.

During fertilization, one reproductive cell joins another. Exactly which reproductive cells will join to become the offspring happens by chance, but it ultimately determines the traits of the offspring. A grid can be used to understand how heredity operates. This grid reveals the mathematical probabilities of observing certain traits. This grid is called a Punnett square. A **Punnett square** can be used to predict all the possible ways in which the alternate alleles can appear.

Homozygous x Homozygous

Pure plants have two identical alleles for each trait. If the two alleles are identical for a trait, the individual is said to be pure or **homozygous** for that trait. If the two alleles are not identical, then the individual is said to be **heterozygous** for that trait.

Traditionally, a capital letter is used for a dominant allele, and a lowercase letter for the recessive allele. Take another look at Mendel's cross between pure (homozygous) tall plants and pure (homozygous) short plants.

The trait for tall stem is represented by the capital letter *T*. Because the plant has two alleles for stem height, the homozygous tall plant is represented by the letters *TT*. The trait for short stem is represented by the lowercase letter *t*. The homozygous short plant is represented by the letters *tt*. A Punnett square can be constructed to show what offspring can be produced. An allele in each male reproductive cell is placed along either the top or the left side of the grid. An allele in each female reproductive cell is placed along either the left side or the top of the grid. The alleles are then combined to show all the possible types of offspring that can be produced.

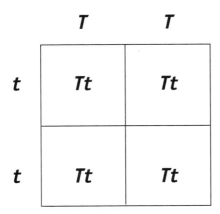

Notice that only offspring with tall stems can be produced. This happens because the allele *T* is dominant over the allele *t*. Therefore, the combination *Tt* in the offspring results in tall stems. Both *TT* and *tt* plants in the P$_1$ generation are homozygous for stem height, while the *Tt* plants in the F$_1$ generation are heterozygous for stem height.

Homozygous x Heterozygous

Now consider what can happen when a homozygous tall (*TT*) plant is crossed with a heterozygous tall (*Tt*) plant.

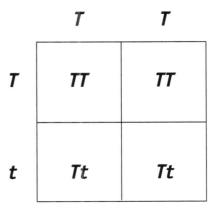

Notice in the above Punnett square that half the offspring will be *TT*, while the other half will be *Tt*. In other words, the probability of homozygous tall (*TT*) offspring is $\frac{2}{4}$ or 50 percent. The probability of heterozygous tall (*Tt*) offspring is also $\frac{2}{4}$ or 50 percent. However, the probability of offspring with tall stems is 100 percent because *T* is dominant over *t*.

Heterozygous x Heterozygous

Now consider what can happen when two heterozygous tall (*Tt*) plants are crossed.

	T	t
T	TT	Tt
t	Tt	tt

Notice in the Punnett square on page 51 that 1 in 4 (25 percent) is expected to be *TT* (tall); 2 in 4 (50 percent) are expected to be *Tt* (tall); and 1 in 4 (25 percent) is expected to be *tt* (short). In this case, the recessive trait can appear in the offspring.

Testcross

Both *TT* and *Tt* plants have tall stems. All these plants have the same appearance, or **phenotype**. However, they do not have the same combination of alleles, or **genotype**. Is there some way to determine what the genotype is of a tall plant—*TT* or *Tt*? The answer can be obtained by performing a testcross. A **testcross** involves crossing an individual with the dominant trait but an unknown genotype (*TT* or *Tt*) with an individual that is homozygous for the recessive trait (*tt*).

Notice that the Punnett square on the left shows that if a plant with tall stems has the genotype *TT*, only plants with tall stems are possible in the offspring. However, the Punnett square on the right shows that if plants with short stems appear in the offspring, the genotype of the parent plant with tall stems must be *Tt*.

Beyond Mendel

Genetics rarely operates as simply as Mendel thought. In some cases, a gene may not have a dominant or recessive allele. In addition, one gene can determine many traits, and one trait can be controlled by many genes. Moreover, genes are not the only factors that determine an organism's traits. The environment also plays a role. A person may have the genes to grow six feet tall. However, the person may not reach that height without a healthy diet.

	T	T
t	Tt	Tt
t	Tt	Tt

	T	t
t	Tt	tt
t	Tt	tt

Lesson 5   Review

Darken the circle for the best answer.

1. Which is the best definition for *genetics*?

   Ⓐ transmission of traits from parents to offspring

   Ⓑ study of dominant and recessive traits

   Ⓒ field of biology that investigates how characteristics are passed from parents to offspring

   Ⓓ cross between two pea plants

2. A guinea pig with black coat color is crossed with a guinea pig with brown coat color. All their offspring have black coat color. Which conclusion can you make from this observation?

   Ⓐ Brown coat color is the dominant trait.

   Ⓑ Black coat color is the dominant trait.

   Ⓒ Black coat color is the recessive trait.

   Ⓓ Neither coat color is a dominant trait.

3. How can you tell whether a trait is dominant or recessive?

   Ⓐ Examine the F1 generation.

   Ⓑ Examine the P1 generation.

   Ⓒ Count the number of organisms produced.

   Ⓓ Find the age of the parent organisms.

4. For certain guinea pigs, black fur (B) is dominant over brown (b) fur. What must be the genotype of a guinea pig with brown fur?

   Ⓐ *BB*   Ⓒ *bb*

   Ⓑ *Bb*   Ⓓ *BB* or *Bb*

5. If the following Punnett square is completed, how many of the four possible outcomes result in a black guinea pig?

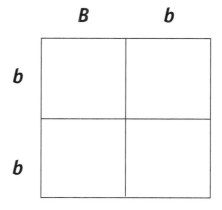

   Ⓐ one   Ⓒ three

   Ⓑ two   Ⓓ four

6. If a child has blond hair and both parents have brown hair, what does that tell you about the allele for blond hair?

   _____

   _____

7. What are two ways in which traits are determined other than those that Mendel discovered?

   _____

   _____

   _____

   _____

   _____

Lesson 5   A Hidden Message

The following terms dealing with genetics are hidden in this word search puzzle. There is also a hidden message. The letters in the message are hidden between the letters of the words in the puzzle. The message reveals a fact about the "father" of genetics. What is the message?

ALLELE	DOMINANT	GENETICS
GENOTYPE	HEREDITY	HETEROZYGOUS
HOMOZYGOUS	OFFSPRING	PHENOTYPE
PUNNETT	RECESSIVE	TESTCROSS

```
H  M  E  N  D  E  L  W  A  E  S  A  M  O  T  G  S  N  K  T
T  E  B  A  F  M  J  V  Y  D  V  C  C  T  H  E  S  W  R  N
E  U  T  M  Y  N  P  Q  T  F  C  I  E  S  H  N  O  S  K  A
L  O  H  E  R  E  D  I  T  Y  F  N  S  X  N  E  R  I  E  N
I  K  F  U  R  Z  R  K  Y  H  N  H  P  S  C  T  C  L  F  I
V  C  S  F  Q  O  D  L  O  U  D  J  E  U  E  I  T  W  Z  M
C  I  T  D  S  N  Z  M  P  P  Q  H  H  X  Y  C  S  E  N  O
A  O  V  L  R  P  O  Y  H  M  L  R  W  M  Z  S  E  L  U  D
J  P  G  R  D  Z  R  E  G  I  C  G  B  X  V  A  T  R  H  Z
O  H  I  L  Y  P  N  I  X  O  I  D  Q  V  W  R  G  U  I  W
Q  L  B  G  T  O  W  Z  N  S  U  B  I  W  U  Z  E  Q  Z  L
I  Q  O  C  T  A  W  K  Y  G  J  S  Q  D  A  P  N  R  X  D
G  U  C  Y  X  V  L  B  S  H  J  M  C  L  E  N  O  U  F  W
S  S  P  E  L  E  L  L  A  O  C  R  A  V  D  L  T  J  B  U
N  E  I  X  K  R  C  B  T  L  R  X  U  Q  G  Y  Y  Z  C  B
H  I  A  S  E  L  W  E  L  G  C  C  F  L  G  P  P  U  K  I
R  Z  F  E  O  I  H  O  S  D  I  O  T  C  C  S  E  S  D  V
N  T  Y  B  W  S  I  I  C  C  F  U  P  J  L  C  D  P  G  L
```

Hidden Message: <WOL>

Lesson 5   A Punnett Square

Use the Punnett square below to answer the questions that follow.

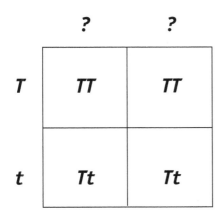

	?	?
T	TT	TT
t	Tt	Tt

1. What is the unknown genotype for one of the parents?

   _____

2. Assume that *T* represents the allele for tall plants and that *t* represents the allele for short plants. What are the phenotypes of the offspring?

   _____

3. Construct a Punnett square to show what offspring are expected if a homozygous plant from the F₁ generation is crossed with a heterozygous plant from the F₁ generation.

4. What two genotypes in the F_1 generation must be crossed to get a plant in the next, or F_2, generation that has a short stem?

   _____

5. Construct a Punnett square to show how the genotypes from your cross in question 4 can produce a plant that has a short stem.

Lesson 5, A Punnett Square
Science 7, SV 9781419034350

Lesson 5

Sickle Cell Anemia

Read the following passage and then answer the questions.

Sickle cell anemia is a genetic disease. People with this condition have red blood cells with an abnormal shape. Normal red blood cells are shaped like a donut but without the holes. Instead of a hole, the red blood cells have a slight depression on each side. This shape allows the cells to flow easily through the blood vessels. The red blood cells in people with sickle cell anemia do not have this rounded shape. Instead, their red blood cells are shaped like a sickle or crescent moon.

Red blood cells transport oxygen to all cells of the body. However, sickle red blood cells cannot transport as much oxygen. In addition, these cells can become trapped in blood vessels. As a result, the blood supply to a part of the body may be cut off.

Sickle cell anemia is caused by a recessive allele. A person must have a recessive allele from each parent to have the disease. A person who is heterozygous for sickle cell anemia does not have the disease. In addition, this person is protected against malaria. Malaria is a disease that is common in countries in Africa where people are more likely to have sickle cell anemia. A person who is heterozygous for sickle cell anemia is somehow protected from malaria.

1. Assume that *S* represents the normal allele and that *s* represents the allele for sickle cell anemia.

   What is the genotype for a person who is heterozygous for sickle cell anemia?

   _____

   What is the genotype of a person who has sickle cell anemia?

   _____

2. Why is it an advantage to be heterozygous for sickle cell anemia rather than have two normal alleles?

   _____

   _____

3. Construct a Punnett square to show what offspring are expected if two people who are heterozygous for sickle cell anemia have children. What are the expected phenotypes of their children?

Lesson 5

Experiment: Making a Pedigree

A genetic trait can be traced through a family tree with the use of a pedigree. A pedigree is a diagram that shows the occurrence of a genetic trait in several generations of a family. The following is an example of a pedigree.

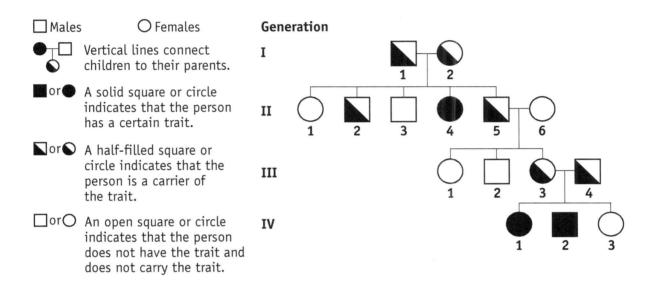

Squares indicate males. Circles represent females. A solid square or circle indicates that the person has a certain trait. A half-filled square or circle indicates that the person has one allele for the trait. An open square or circle indicates that the person does not have the trait and does not carry the trait. Horizontal lines that connect a square and a circle indicate the parents. Vertical lines connect the parents to their children. For example, individuals 1 and 2 are two parents. They have five children, represented by numbers 1–5. Individual number 5 is a male who has three children with individual number 6.

In the following experiment, you will construct a pedigree of your family by checking for a genetic trait that is easy to spot. For purposes of this experiment, assume that the trait is controlled by a dominant allele. Keep in mind, however, that very few, if any, traits in humans are controlled the same way as Mendel observed in pea plants.

Experiment: Making a Pedigree (cont'd.)

You Will Need

pencil
paper

Procedure

1. Stick out your tongue and see if you can curl it or roll it into the shape of a cylinder.

2. Check as many family members as possible to see if they are tongue "rollers" or "nonrollers."

3. Construct a pedigree to show how this trait is inherited in your family.

Results and Analysis

1. How many members of your family are tongue "rollers"? How many are "nonrollers"?

_____

2. Assume that the ability to roll the tongue is determined by a dominant allele represented by the letter *T*. What genotypes can a "roller" have?

_____

3. If a father cannot roll his tongue but has a daughter who can roll her tongue, what does this tell you about the child's genotype?

_____

_____

Conclusion

What conclusion can you draw from your results?

_____

_____

Lesson 6 Regulation and Behavior

An organism must regulate its internal environment. For example, human body temperature is regulated so that it stabilizes at around 98.6°F. If the body temperature begins to drop, then processes are set in motion to raise it. If the body temperature begins to rise, then processes are set in motion to lower it. To regulate its internal environment, an organism must have some way of sensing internal conditions. In other words, the human body must have some way of knowing its internal temperature. In this lesson, you will learn how the human body senses its internal conditions and responds to maintain a stable internal environment.

Homeostasis

Have you ever walked outdoors and found that it was colder than you expected? Your first thought may have been to go back inside and get a sweater or coat. But then your body did not feel as cold. Your body got used to the cold because of homeostasis. **Homeostasis** is the maintenance of a constant internal environment despite changes in the external environment. When you went outside, homeostasis helped you get used to the cold. How did this happen?

First, you became aware that it was cold. You learned about various organ systems in Lesson 4.

Another organ system is the nervous system. The most important organ in this system is the brain. The brain is constantly receiving information from all parts of the body. These include temperature sensors in the skin. These temperature sensors are specialized nerve cells that respond to hot and cold. Cold weather activates the cold sensors. These sensors send signals

Key Terms

homeostasis—the maintenance of a constant internal environment despite changes in the external environment

cerebrum—the part of the brain that controls voluntary responses and functions in memory and reasoning

cerebellum—the part of the brain that coordinates muscle action

medulla—the part of the brain that controls involuntary responses

endocrine system—the organ system that secretes hormones to regulate body functions

hormone—a chemical messenger that is made in one part of the body that causes a change in another part of the body

negative feedback—a system where a movement in one direction triggers a response in the opposite direction

insulin—a hormone that lowers the blood sugar level

glucagon—a hormone that raises the blood sugar level

to the brain. The brain interprets these signals and informs the body that it is cold outside.

Signals are then sent by the brain to various parts of the body. Blood vessels near the surface of the body are instructed to constrict or become narrower. This reduces blood flow to parts of the body near the surface. By reducing blood flow, less heat is lost through the skin.

Signals are also sent to muscles, which are instructed to start moving quickly. As a result, the body may start to shiver. Shivering produces heat that makes the body feel warmer. Therefore, the nervous, circulatory, and muscular systems all work together in homeostasis. As a result, you did not feel as cold as when you first went outside.

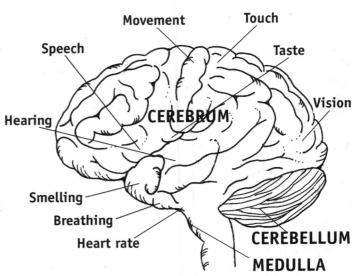

The Cerebrum

The largest part of the brain is the **cerebrum.** The cerebrum controls voluntary responses. As you can see in the illustration above, the cerebrum also collects and interprets information from the senses, such as hearing, smell, taste, and sight. The cerebrum is also the center of memory and reasoning. It allows us to solve problems, interpret emotions, learn language, process information, write poetry, create art, and play music.

The Brain

The brain is the main control center of the nervous system. The brain is responsible for processing information and sending out signals so that the proper actions are taken. Some of these processes happen automatically. In other words, you do not think about making them happen. These responses are called involuntary. Shivering is an involuntary response. You don't think about shivering when you are cold. You just do it automatically.

Other responses controlled by the brain are voluntary. For example, you may decide to put on a coat when you are cold. Or you may decide to go back indoors where it is warmer. These responses are called voluntary.

The brain has three main parts—the cerebrum, the cerebellum, and the medulla. Each part plays a role in maintaining homeostasis.

The Cerebellum

The second largest part of the brain is the cerebellum. As you can see in the above illustration, the cerebellum lies beneath the back of the cerebrum. The **cerebellum** coordinates the actions of muscles and bones. For example, you may have stumbled when walking outdoors on that cold day. Your cerebellum kept you from falling.

Information from various parts of your body is constantly being sent to the cerebellum. The cerebellum interprets this information to keep track of the position of each part of the body. When the cerebellum senses that the body is out of balance and might stumble or fall, it sends out signals to muscles to contract. Those contractions shift a person's weight and keep the person from falling.

The Medulla

The medulla is the part of the brain that connects to the spinal cord. The **medulla** controls involuntary processes. For example, the medulla controls heart rate and body temperature. Like the cerebrum and cerebellum, the medulla is constantly receiving information. This information is interpreted, and the appropriate signals are then sent out.

Consider what happens when a person is running. The medulla receives information that body cells require more oxygen to supply energy for the muscles to move. The medulla will then send signals to the heart to make it beat faster. 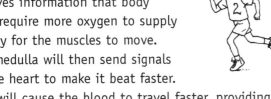 This will cause the blood to travel faster, providing more oxygen to the cells. The cells can then supply the energy the muscles need to contract.

The Endocrine System

The nervous system is not the only system that regulates body functions. The **endocrine system** also controls body functions. However, the endocrine system does not use signals that are sent along a network of cells like the nervous system does. Rather, the endocrine system uses special chemicals known as hormones. A **hormone** is a chemical messenger that is made in one part of the body that causes a change in another part of the body. Hormones are transported through the body by the blood.

The endocrine system operates with the help of a control system called negative feedback. **Negative feedback** is a system where a movement in one direction triggers a response in the opposite direction. An example of negative feedback can be seen in thermostats that are used to control the temperature in homes and offices.

Assume that the thermostat is set to 68°F. If the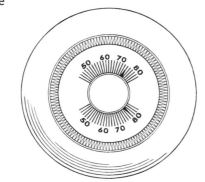

temperature drops below this value, then the thermostat will turn on the heating system. Once the temperature reaches 68°F, then the thermostat will shut off the system. This on-off cycle continues to maintain the temperature inside the house at 68°F. This is how homeostasis operates inside the body. One example is the control of the blood sugar level.

Blood Sugar Levels

Cells use a sugar called glucose as their primary source of energy. Glucose must be continuously supplied to all cells. Glucose is obtained from the digestion of starches. You learned in Lesson 4 that digested materials are absorbed in the small intestine. Glucose is one of these digested materials that is absorbed into the bloodstream from the small intestine.

After the digested materials have been absorbed, the level of glucose in the blood may be high. If so, an organ called the pancreas releases a hormone known as insulin into the blood. **Insulin** is a hormone that lowers the level of sugar in the blood. Insulin signals the liver to remove glucose from the blood and store it. The liver stores the excess glucose as a substance called glycogen. Once the excess glucose has been removed from the blood, the pancreas stops releasing insulin.

If the blood sugar level falls too low, the pancreas starts releasing another hormone called glucagon. **Glucagon** is a hormone that raises the blood sugar level. Glucagon tells the liver to break down glycogen into glucose. The liver then releases the glucose into the bloodstream. As a result, the blood sugar level increases. Therefore, both insulin and glucagon work to keep the level of glucose in the blood within a certain range. Failure to regulate the blood sugar level can result in a disease called diabetes. A person who has diabetes may need daily injections of insulin to keep his or her blood sugar levels within normal limits.

The following figure illustrates how your endocrine system uses negative feedback to control your blood-glucose level.

5b Sometimes, to raise your blood-glucose level, you must eat something.

1 Glucose is fuel for your body. Glucose is absorbed into the bloodstream from the small intestine.

5a If your blood-glucose level falls too low, glucagon tells the liver to break down glycogen and release the glucose into your blood.

2 When the glucose level in the blood is high, such as after a meal, the pancreas releases the hormone insulin into the blood.

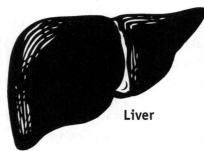

Pancreas

Pancreas

4 When the pancreas detects that your blood-glucose level has returned to normal, it stops releasing insulin.

3 Insulin signals the liver to take in glucose from the blood, convert the glucose into glycogen, and to store glycogen for future energy neeeds.

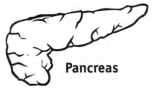

Liver

Lesson 6   Review

Darken the circle for the best answer.

1. Which structure controls involuntary actions?

   (A) pancreas

   (B) cerebrum

   (C) cerebellum

   (D) medulla

2. Which of the following is part of the endocrine system?

   (A) muscles

   (B) hormones

   (C) blood

   (D) glucose

3. A hormone imbalance may result in

   (A) homeostasis.

   (B) loss of balance.

   (C) diabetes.

   (D) negative feedback control.

4. Hormone production is regulated by

   (A) a negative feedback system.

   (B) temperature.

   (C) the cerebrum.

   (D) the liver.

5. Epinephrine is another hormone that increases the blood sugar level. How would epinephrine affect the body?

   (A) It would have the opposite effect of glucagon.

   (B) It would decrease energy production by the cells.

   (C) It would have the opposite effect of insulin.

   (D) It would not have any effect on the body.

6. Which of the following is an involuntary process?

   (A) doing homework

   (B) reading a book

   (C) digesting food

   (D) running fast

7. Explain why the endocrine system is important to your body.

   _____

   _____

   _____

8. What would happen to blood sugar levels if negative feedback mechanisms were not working?

   _____

   _____

   _____

Lesson 6   How Hot Can It Get?

Read the following passage and then answer the questions.

How hot can it get before you start to feel uncomfortable? Perhaps you start to perspire. You may also get thirsty. The temperature may get so high that you look for a place that is air-conditioned. In the 1770s, a British scientist named Charles Blagden decided to see how hot it could get before he felt uncomfortable.

Blagden convinced two friends to join him in an unusual experiment. They went into a small room where the temperature had been raised to about 260°F. They knew that water boils at 212°F, so they were aware that they could really say that the temperature inside the room was "boiling hot." The three men also took a dog and a steak with them inside the room.

The three men stood most of time, frequently walking about the room. Blagden later wrote that the three of them did not feel "any great discomfort." When Blagden took his temperature, he observed that it was only one degree above normal. After about 45 minutes, the three men and the dog came out of the room. Not only were they all alive, they also felt fine. Before they left the room, the men checked on the steak. They observed that the steak was cooked.

1. What evidence did Blagden obtain to show that his body was maintaining homeostasis despite the high temperature?

_____

_____

2. Why do you think that Blagden asked two friends to join him in this experiment?

_____

_____

_____

3. What proof could Blagden provide to show how hot it had been inside the room?

_____

_____

_____

4. Why do you think Blagden took a dog inside the room?

_____

_____

_____

5. What would Blagden have observed if he had taken a bowl of water with him inside the room?

_____

_____

Lesson 6

Blood Sugar Levels

The following table shows the results obtained by a person monitoring blood sugar levels after eating lunch at noon. Use the information in this table to answer the questions that follow.

Blood Glucose	
Time tested	Blood-glucose level (mg/1,000 mL)
1:00 P.M.	178
2:00 P.M.	112
3:00 P.M.	100
4:00 P.M.	89

1. Which hormone was being produced shortly after 1:00 P.M.? Explain your answer.

_____

_____

2. What was the average hourly decrease in the blood sugar level?

_____

_____

3. Predict what the blood sugar level will be at 5:00 P.M.

_____

_____

4. Assume that the person does not eat dinner. What hormone do you expect would start to be produced at some point during the night? Explain your answer.

_____

_____

Lesson 6   Experiment: Perspiration

A person perspires on hot days. This is one way the body maintains a stable internal temperature. The perspiration, or sweat, that collects on the skin evaporates. In the following experiment, you will learn how the evaporation of sweat cools the body.

You Will Need

thermometer
pencil
paper
cotton ball
rubbing alcohol

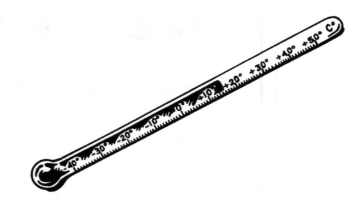

Procedure

1. Allow the thermometer to adjust to room temperature. Record the temperature on a sheet of paper.

2. Dip the cotton ball in rubbing alcohol.

3. Pull apart the cotton ball to make a sheet of cotton.

4. Wrap the cotton sheet around the bulb of the thermometer.

5. Blow on the cotton so that the alcohol evaporates.

6. Record the temperature after all the alcohol has evaporated.

Results and Analysis

What happens to the temperature as the alcohol evaporates?

_____

_____

Conclusion

What conclusion can you draw based on your observations?

_____

_____

Lesson 7 Populations and Ecosystems

All organisms interact with their environment, which includes both living and nonliving things. Because the environment is so complex, scientists divide it into different levels. In this lesson, you will learn about these different levels, from the simplest to the most complex.

From Organisms to Biomes

The simplest level in any environment is an individual organism. The next level is the species. A **species** consists of organisms that have common features and can mate with one another. For example, all the robins that you may see in spring and summer belong to a species called *Turdus migratorius*. Any member of this species can mate with a robin of the opposite sex to produce more robins.

All the robins that live in a particular area, such as your neighborhood, make up the next level known as a population. A **population** consists of all the members of the same species that live in the same place.

The next level is a community. A **community** includes different populations that live in the same place. For example, a community includes the robins, irises, honeybees, mockingbirds, and all the other organisms that live in your neighborhood. Notice that a community includes only living things.

The next level includes both living and nonliving things. This is an ecosystem. An **ecosystem** consists of all the organisms within a community and the nonliving things with which they interact, such as air, water, and soil.

The next level is a biome. A **biome** is a region that contains groups of similar ecosystems and

climates. There are several major biomes that can be grouped into three larger categories: terrestrial biomes, marine biomes, and freshwater biomes.

To summarize, the following represents the levels that scientists use to describe the environment, starting with the simplest.

organism → species → population → community → ecosystem → biome

Terrestrial Biomes

Land biomes, also known as **terrestrial biomes**, include several different types of regions. One is a

Key Terms

species—a group of organisms that have common features and can mate with one another

population—all the members of the same species that live in the same place

community—the different populations that live in the same place

ecosystem—all the organisms within a community and the nonliving things with which they interact

biome—a region that contains groups of similar ecosystems and climates

terrestrial biome—a land biome

permafrost—a layer of permanently frozen soil under the surface

adaptation—a trait or behavior that increases an organism's chances of survival

temperate deciduous forest. This biome is made up of deciduous trees that lose their leaves in the fall. These trees include the birch, beech, maple, oak, hickory, elm, willow, and cottonwood. Animals include bears, deer, rabbits, squirrels, and many species of birds. Summers are warm, while winters are cold.

Another terrestrial biome is a coniferous forest. This biome is made up of trees that do not lose their leaves in cold weather. These trees, which have needles, include the pine, fir, hemlock, and spruce. Animals include moose, bears, lynx, and wolves. Snow covers the ground during the long winters.

A tropical rain forest biome is made up of tall trees with broad leaves that form dense vegetation. As many as 300 species of trees can be found in an area the size of two football fields. These trees form what is commonly called a jungle. Animals include a variety of snakes and lizards, colorful birds, and many kinds of monkeys.

A grassland biome is made up of grasses mixed with plants that produce colorful flowers. In the United States, this biome is commonly called a prairie. This biome has rich, fertile soil, making it well suited for growing crops. Animals include bison, mice, and prairie dogs.

A desert biome is made up of land that receives very little rainfall throughout the year. As a result, vegetation is sparse and consists mostly of cactus plants. Animals include snakes, lizards, and jack rabbits.

A tundra biome is characterized by very cold conditions and very little vegetation. A permanently frozen layer of soil under the surface, known as **permafrost**, is present only in the tundra. This biome is found in the far north and near the tops of tall mountains. Animals include musk, wolves, and oxen.

The following table summarizes the main features of the terrestrial biomes.

Terrestrial biome	Average yearly temperature range	Average yearly precipitation	Soil	Vegetation
Temperate deciduous forest	43°F to 82°F	30–50 inches	moist with moderate nutrients	broad-leafed trees and shrubs
Coniferous forest	−14°F to 57°F	14–30 inches	acidic with low nutrient content	evergreen trees
Tropical rain forest	68°F to 93°F	79–158 inches	moist with low nutrient content	broad-leafed trees
Grassland	32°F to 77°F	10–30 inches	deep layer of topsoil rich in nutrients	grasses
Desert	44°F to 100°F	less than 10 inches	dry, sandy with few nutrients	cactuses
Tundra	−15°F to 63°F	less than 10 inches	thin layer over permafrost	mosses, lichens

Marine Biomes

The marine biome consists of the oceans, which cover almost 75 percent of Earth's surface. There are four distinct zones in a marine biome. The region where an ocean meets the land is called the *intertidal zone*. Animals include clams, mussels, and oysters that move in and out of their shells as the tide moves in and out.

The next zone found moving away from shore is called the *neritic zone*. The neritic zone contains more species and numbers of organisms than any other zone. Numerous fishes, sea turtles, and squid live in this zone. Coral reefs are found in the neritic zone of tropical waters.

The open ocean that is made up of deep water is the *oceanic zone*. Because sunlight cannot penetrate more than 650 feet through ocean water, most of this zone is cold, dark, and does not support much life. Animals include fishes and whales. Bacteria live near deep-sea thermal vents which lie more than 8000 feet below sea level and where the temperature exceeds 1400°F.

The ocean floor is called the *benthic zone*. Near the shore, the benthic zone may be shallow enough for light to penetrate. In the open ocean, the benthic zone may lie far beneath the surface where no light reaches. Most animals are not permanent residents of the benthic zone. They usually swim or move toward the surface. The benthic zone contains some unusual creatures such as the one shown below.

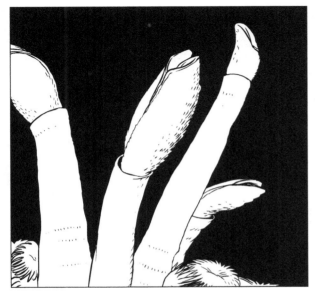

Giant Tube Worms

Freshwater Biomes

Freshwater biomes include lakes and ponds that consist of still water that may or not be connected to flowing water. Some of these biomes may contain dense vegetation that makes the water murky. Rivers and streams consist of running water that flows toward the oceans. The place where a river or stream meets the ocean forms still another biome called an estuary. The amount of salt in the water of an estuary is always changing. Therefore, animals and plants that live in estuaries must be able to tolerate the constantly changing salt conditions.

Adaptations

In the nineteenth century, an English scientist named Charles Darwin recognized that certain organisms were better equipped to survive in their environments. These organisms possess the necessary adaptations. An **adaptation** is a trait or behavior that increases an organism's chances of survival.

Adaptations depend on the environment in which an organism lives. Consider the example of a tundra and rain forest. The white fur of the artic hare is an adaptation. The white fur helps the hare blend into its snowy background and avoid being eaten by some other organism. However, the white fur would not help the hare in the lush green background of a tropical rain forest. Rather, its white fur would make it an easy target.

Survival in a Tundra Biome

Survival is always a challenge. However, conditions in some biomes such as a tundra can be quite harsh, making survival more challenging than it is in other biomes. To overcome this challenge, tundra organisms have developed some interesting and unusual adaptations.

An example is the *Kobresia*, a plant that grows in the Arctic tundra. This plant grows very quickly to take advantage of the extremely short growing season. However, *Kobresia* gets no taller than a person's hand. Its short height keeps it from being thrashed around by the strong winds. This plant can absorb water from the ground much faster than other plants. It can also absorb nutrients that other plants cannot. These are adaptations that allow *Kobresia* to grow in the nutrient-poor soil of the tundra. Because of its adaptations, a *Kobresia* plant can live for more than 200 years in one of the harshest biomes.

Animals in the tundra are also well adapted. One of the most interesting adaptations to the arctic cold can be seen in a primary consumer known as the woolly bear. Despite its name, this animal is not a bear but a caterpillar that grows to be about the size of your thumb. During the winter, the woolly bear produces chemicals that act like antifreeze to prevent ice from forming inside its body. During cold weather, the wooly bear remains inactive. It awakens to grow just a little bit during one month in summer. This cycle continues for 14 years until the caterpillar is finally large enough to change into a moth.

Lesson 7   Review

Darken the circle by the best answer.

1. Which of these is an example of a terrestrial biome?

   (A) river

   (B) estuary

   (C) tundra

   (D) lake

2. Approximately how much of Earth is covered by terrestrial biomes?

   (A) 75%

   (B) 50%

   (C) 25%

   (D) one-third

3. Photosynthesis is the process organisms use to convert light energy into nutrients, such as sugars. Why are photosynthetic organisms found only near the surface of the oceanic zone?

   (A) They are too light to sink deeper.

   (B) This region of the ocean is very shallow.

   (C) Large organisms near the ocean floor eat them.

   (D) Sunlight penetrates only a few hundred feet into the oceanic zone.

4. Which correctly shows the order of organization?

   (A) organism → species → population → community → ecosystem → biome

   (B) organism → species → community → population → ecosystem → biome

   (C) species → organism → population → community → biome → ecosystem

   (D) organism → population → species → community → ecosystem → biome

5. How does an adaptation benefit an organism?

   (A) It guarantees that the organism will survive.

   (B) It increases an organism's chances of survival.

   (C) It allows an organism to move from one biome to another.

   (D) It decreases the chances that the organism will reproduce.

6. Over time, the available water in the soil of a particular biome decreases. Which adaptation is *most likely* to allow a plant to survive in this soil?

   (A) taller plants

   (B) plants with shorter roots

   (C) plants that require less water

   (D) plants with larger flowers

Review (cont'd.)

~~~~~~

7. Assume that a plant lives on the ground in a tropical forest where the dense canopy blocks sunlight from reaching the lower layers. Which adaptation would *most likely* help the ground plant to survive?

   Ⓐ wide, flat leaves

   Ⓑ shorter trunk

   Ⓒ thick roots

   Ⓓ thinner branches

8. Many fish that live in the deep ocean produce light. How might this be an adaptation in this region of an ocean biome?

_____

_____

_____

_____

_____

9. Why are so few types of plants able to grow in the tundra?

_____

_____

_____

_____

_____

Lesson 7   Biomes of Australia

The map below shows the biomes of Australia. Use this map to answer the questions that follow.

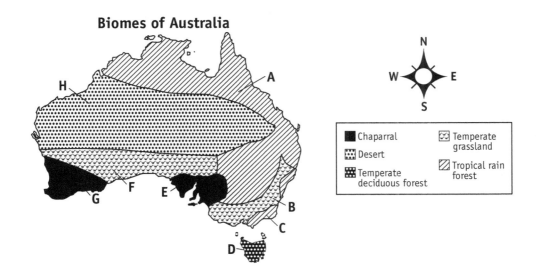

Biomes of Australia

1. Which letter represents a biome where cactus plants are the main vegetation?

   (A) A
   (B) D
   (C) F
   (D) H

2. Which letter represents a biome that receives the highest average yearly precipitation?

   (A) A
   (B) E
   (C) F
   (D) G

3. Which letter represents a biome where the trees lose their leaves during part of the year?

   (A) A
   (B) B
   (C) C
   (D) D

4. Which letters represent a biome where the soil is rich in nutrients and good for growing crops?

   (A) A and C
   (B) B and F
   (C) C and H
   (D) D and G

Lesson 7   Deep Below the Surface

Read the following passage and then answer the questions that follow the passage.

Jacques Piccard could not believe what he saw. A fish that looked like a flounder swam by and then quickly disappeared. Seeing a fish that looks like a flounder may not seem that unusual. However, Piccard was on the ocean bottom, almost seven miles beneath the surface. No one had thought that anything could live that deep down in the ocean. The flounder-like fish was only one of several living things Piccard saw.

On January 23, 1960, Piccard and Don Walsh took a United States Navy vessel named *Trieste* to the deepest spot on Earth. This spot is the Marianas Trench in the Pacific Ocean. The Marianas Trench lies just east of the Philippine Islands. To appreciate how deep this trench is, imagine that Mount Everest rose from the bottom of the Marianas Trench. Mount Everest is the highest point on land. If Mount Everest rose from the Marianas Trench, there would still be one mile of water above its top!

The *Trieste* looks like a submarine, but it is actually a vessel called a bathyscaph. The word *bathyscaph* comes from two Greek words that mean "deep boat." A bathyscaph is built to dive deep into the ocean where the pressure is enormous. While in the Marianas Trench, the pressure on the *Trieste* was more than one thousand times greater than it was at sea level.

More than 40 years have passed since Piccard and Walsh set the world's record for the deepest dive. In fact, no one has even come close to their record. These two men are still the only ones who have ever visited the deepest part of the ocean.

1. What surprised Piccard and Walsh during their visit to the Marianas Trench?

   _____

   _____

2. Why didn't Piccard and Walsh visit the Marianas Trench in a submarine?

   _____

   _____

3. What zone of the ocean biome did Piccard and Walsh visit?

   _____

   _____

4. Describe two adaptations that any organism in this zone must have to survive.

   _____

   _____

Lesson 7   Precipitation in a Biome

Use the graph below to answer the questions that follow.

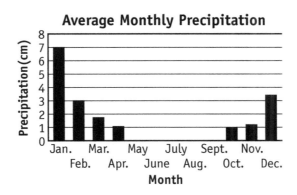

1. How many centimeters (cm) of rain fell in this region during the course of the year?

_____

2. Which two biomes might be found in the region described in the above graph? Explain the reason for your choices. (Note: Use the conversion factor 1 in. = 2.54 cm.)

_____

_____

_____

3. The average monthly temperature never drops below freezing in the region described in the above graph. Based on this information, can you identify which biome is most likely found in this region? Explain your answer.

_____

_____

_____

4. Name three animals that you might find in this biome.

_____

_____

Lesson 7   Experiment: Making a Balanced Ecosystem

You learned that an ecosystem consists of both living and nonliving factors in an environment. In this experiment, you will establish an ecosystem and observe how organisms interact with these factors. These interactions are important to maintain a balanced ecosystem. You will have to make observations on your ecosystem for a period of at least two weeks.

You Will Need

large pot
three large jars with lids
four aquarium fish or snails
aquatic plants, such as *Anacharus*
three aquarium thermometers

Procedure

1. Fill a large pot with water and allow it to sit for at least 24 hours. This will allow any gases that might harm the organisms to escape.

2. Use the aged water to fill the three jars within one inch of their tops.

3. Place two fish or snails in the first jar. Also place an aquarium thermometer in the jar. Place the lid on the jar securely.

4. Place two sprigs of the aquatic plant in a second jar. Also place a thermometer in the jar and seal it.

5. Place two sprigs of the aquatic plant and two fish or snails in the third jar. Again place a thermometer in the jar and seal it.

 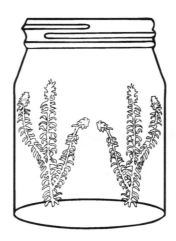 

Experiment: Making a Balanced Ecosystem (cont'd.)

6. Place the jars in an area where they can remain undisturbed for at least two weeks. Try to keep the water temperature around 70°F.

7. Observe your ecosystems each day for the next two weeks. Record your observations, such as the water temperature in each jar, how active the animals are, and whether the plants show any signs of growth.

8. IMPORTANT: If the animals in either of the two jars show any signs of distress, immediately open the jar and remove them. Place them in aged water in an open jar.

Results and Analysis

1. Where does a fish or snail get its food?

_____

2. Where does the oxygen come from that the animals need to survive?

_____

3. The plants need carbon dioxide to make food in photosynthesis. Where does the plant get this carbon dioxide?

_____

_____

Conclusion

What conclusion can you draw based upon your observations?

_____

_____

_____

Lesson 8 Diversity and Adaptations of Organisms

In 1831, a young Englishman named Charles Darwin began a five-year voyage around the world. The ship he traveled on was called the *Beagle*. Darwin had signed on as the ship's naturalist, which is a scientist who studies nature. During this long voyage, Darwin collected thousands of plant and animal specimens. He was amazed at some of the unusual organisms he observed. For example, Darwin was impressed by the giant tortoises on the Galápagos Islands, which lie about 600 miles west of Ecuador in South America. These animals can live almost 100 years, weigh as much as 400 pounds, and grow to nearly 6 feet in length. But what really amazed Darwin was the tremendous diversity of life that exists on Earth. Yet, all this diversity of life has something in common, as you will learn in this lesson.

Common Ancestors

Across Earth, there are millions of different species. All these organisms point to the biodiversity that exists on Earth. **Biodiversity** is the variety and complexity of life that inhabits Earth. This biodiversity ranges from single-cell organisms to complex living things made of trillions of cells, such as humans.

Scientists think that all living species descended from common ancestors. This includes *Homo sapiens*, the species to which modern humans belong. When Darwin returned to England after his long voyage, he thought about how species change over time. He recognized that some species show striking similarities. For example, humans share certain characteristics with apes and monkeys. These

Key Terms

biodiversity—the variety and complexity of life that exists on Earth

primate—a mammal with an opposable thumb and three-dimensional vision

hominid—a primate that walks upright

bipedalism—the ability to walk upright

homologous features—similar features that arose in a common ancestor but perform different functions in different organisms

vestigial structure—a structure that has no known function but likely functioned in some ancestor of modern organisms

embryo—an early stage of development of a plant or animal

hemoglobin—a chemical compound that transports oxygen in the blood

deoxyribonucleic acid (DNA)—a chemical compound that stores hereditary information

organisms are known as primates. A **primate** is a mammal that has an opposable thumb for grasping objects and three-dimensional vision because both eyes are located at the front of the head.

Other features that primates share include color vision and flattened nails rather than claws. Color vision may have arisen when primates became more active during the day than at night. All these primate features arose as adaptations over a long period of time.

Many people believe Darwin claimed that humans descended from monkeys or apes. He never said or wrote such a thing. Rather, Darwin stated that humans, apes, and monkeys share a common ancestor. Scientists think that this ancestor lived more than 45 million years ago. Scientists also think that the chimpanzee, a type of ape, is the closest living relative of humans. Humans and chimpanzees share a common ancestor that lived between 5 million and 30 million years ago. At that point, the ancestors of humans and apes began to evolve along different lines.

Hominids

Today, humans are in a family separate from other primates. This family is called **hominids.** Only humans and their human-like ancestors are classified as hominids. The main characteristic that separates hominids from other primates is the ability to walk upright. This is known as **bipedalism.** A comparison of the skeletons of a gorilla and a human shows why only humans exhibit bipedalism.

Notice that the human skeleton is built so that a person can walk upright. The hipbone, or pelvis, is upright and helps hold the entire skeleton upright. In contrast, a gorilla's pelvis is tilted. As a result, its

large rib cage, heavy neck, and head bend forward. The long arms provide balance on the ground as the gorilla walks on its arms and legs.

Comparing Skeletal Structures

Comparing primate skeletons reveals striking similarities among humans, apes, and monkeys. These similarities suggest a common ancestor. However, comparing primate skeletal structures with other organisms such as cats, dolphins, and bats suggest that all these organisms have a common ancestor. Consider a human's arm, a dolphin's flipper, a cat's leg, and a bat's wing. On the surface, these structures do not look alike. However, if you take a closer look under the surface, a striking similarity appears. The structure and order of bones of a human arm are similar to those of the front limbs of a dolphin, cat, and bat.

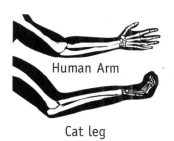

Human Arm

Cat leg

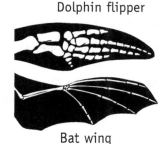

Dolphin flipper

Bat wing

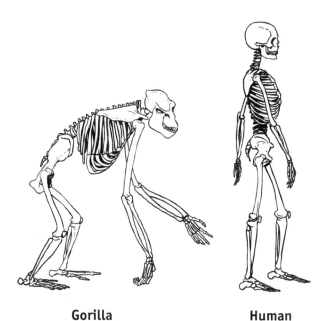

Gorilla   **Human**

The similarities in these bones suggest that humans, dolphins, cats, and bats had a common ancestor. Over many millions of years, changes occurred in the limb bones of the descendants of this common ancestor. Eventually the bones performed different functions in each type of animal. A dolphin's flipper helps it swim, a cat's leg helps it walk, run, and jump. A bat's wing helps it fly. A human arm performs many functions. Similar features that arose in a common ancestor but perform different functions are called **homologous features**.

Vestigial Structures

Humans have an appendix, which is a small, fingerlike structure attached to the intestine. The appendix has no known function. A structure that has no known function is called a **vestigial structure**. A vestigial structure was useful to an ancestor of a modern organism but has lost that function over time.

A vestigial structure in a modern organism is evidence that the structure was functional in some ancestor of the modern organism. In addition, an organism with a vestigial structure probably shares a common ancestor with an organism that has a working version of the same structure. Consider the example of modern whales.

Whales do not have hind limbs. However, they do have tiny hip bones. In addition, some sperm whales have vestigial leg bones. Some even have tiny bumps that protrude from their body where hind limbs would be. Scientists think that these hip bones were inherited from the whales' four-legged ancestors. This ancestor was probably a mammal that lived on land and could run on four legs. A more recent ancestor was probably a mammal that spent time both on land and in water. Descendants of these ancestors include modern whales and four-legged land animals such as pigs, bison, and hippopotamuses. The vestigial hip bones in whales suggest that all these animals share a common ancestor.

Comparing Embryos

An early stage of development of a plant or animal is known as an **embryo**. When studying the embryos of different animals, scientists discovered something unusual. The embryos of certain animals are very similar. For example, in their early stages, the embryos of a fish, rabbit, and gorilla look quite similar.

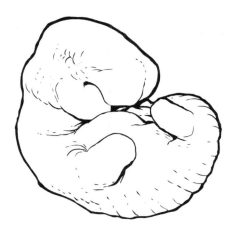

Embryo

As the embryos develop, these similarities slowly disappear. Nevertheless, the similarities in the early stages of their development represent another piece of evidence that organisms share a common ancestor.

Comparing Chemical Compounds

Another line of evidence for common ancestors comes from a study of chemical compounds in different organisms. For example, many species have a chemical compound called hemoglobin. **Hemoglobin** is a protein that transports oxygen in the blood. Like all proteins, hemoglobin is made of building blocks called amino acids. These amino acids are arranged in a specific order to make a protein such as hemoglobin.

The amino acid sequences in human and gorilla hemoglobin differ by only one amino acid. This similarity is very striking when you consider that hemoglobin is made from 574 amino acids. In contrast, the hemoglobin of humans and frogs differs by 67 amino acids. This suggests that more time has passed since humans and frogs shared a common ancestor than has passed since humans and gorillas shared a common ancestor.

Another chemical compound that has been compared in different species is **deoxyribonucleic acid**, abbreviated DNA. DNA stores the hereditary information. Traits are inherited as a result of coded instructions contained in an organism's DNA. Therefore, if two species share a common ancestor, then their DNAs should be similar.

The DNA of a house cat is more similar to the DNA of a tiger than it is to the DNA of a dog. This suggests that a house cat and a tiger share a common ancestor who lived more recently in the past than did the common ancestor to cats, tigers, and dogs.

Like proteins, DNA is made from smaller building blocks. In the case of DNA, these building blocks are called bases. The DNAs in both humans and chimps are made from about three billion bases. Amazingly, their DNAs differ by only slightly more than 1 percent. This striking similarity is additional evidence that humans and chimpanzees share a common ancestor. The fact that all existing species have DNA as their hereditary material supports the theory that all species share a common ancestor.

Lesson 8   Review

Darken the circle by the best answer.

1. Some snakes have tiny pelvic and limb bones. These bones are examples of
   - (A) homologous features.
   - (B) the embryo stage of development.
   - (C) vestigial structures.
   - (D) how DNA functions to carry the hereditary information.

2. If two organisms share a common ancestor, then they
   - (A) must belong to the same species.
   - (B) must have identical DNAs.
   - (C) are no longer alive today.
   - (D) have a relationship with an extinct organism.

3. The forelimbs of an alligator and the flipper of a penguin are homologous structures. Therefore, these forelimbs
   - (A) have the same function.
   - (B) have very similar skeletal structures.
   - (C) are not used by either organism.
   - (D) show that these two organisms do not share a common ancestor.

4. What discovery did Charles Darwin make as a result of the observations he made during his long voyage around the world?
   - (A) Modern organisms share a common ancestor.
   - (B) The hereditary information of an organism is stored in DNA.
   - (C) Humans descended from the apes.
   - (D) The appendix is a vestigial structure.

5. What is the main characteristic that separates hominids from other animals?
   - (A) large brain
   - (B) opposable thumb
   - (C) bipedalism
   - (D) three-dimensional vision

6. A feature that helps an organism survive is known as a(n)
   - (A) adaptation.
   - (B) skeletal structure.
   - (C) fossil.
   - (D) homologous structure.

Review (cont'd.)

7. Which are likely to have DNA that is more alike—siblings or cousins? Explain your answer.

siblings because same parents

8. Describe two ways that organisms can be compared to provide evidence that they have a common ancestor.

DNA and skeletal structures

Lesson 8   A Common Ancestor

The diagram below is a model of a proposed relationship between ancient and modern mammals. Use this model to answer the questions that follow.

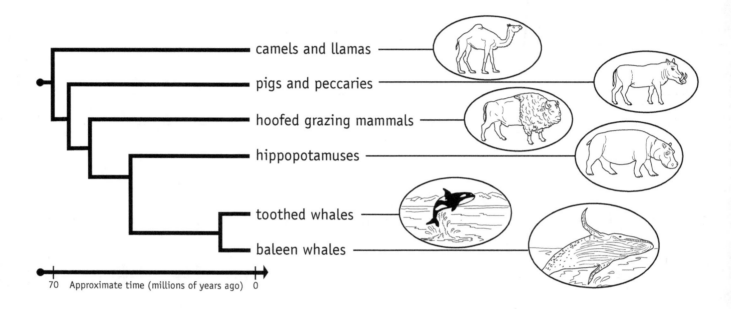

camels and llamas

pigs and peccaries

hoofed grazing mammals

hippopotamuses

toothed whales

baleen whales

70   Approximate time (millions of years ago)   0

1. Which organisms share a common ancestor that lived most recently?

_____

2. About how long ago did the common ancestor to all the organisms in the model above live?

_____

3. Which organisms were the first to branch off from this common ancestor?

_____

4. Which organisms share the most recent common ancestor with toothed and baleen whales?

_____

5. Which animals share the most recent common ancestor with hoofed grazing mammals?

_____

Lesson 8   Humans and Apes

The figure below shows a possible ancestral relationship between humans and modern apes. The time scale represents millions of years (mya). Use this figure to answer the questions that follow.

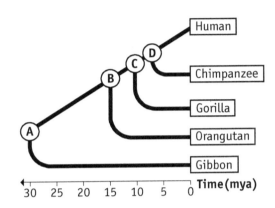

1. Which letter represents the ancestor of all the apes? How long ago did this ancestor live?

_____

2. Which letter represents the common ancestor to humans and chimpanzees? How long ago did this ancestor live according to the diagram above?

_____

3. To which living ape are gorillas most closely related?

_____

4. Which organisms share the common ancestor represented by the letter B?

_____

_____

5. Would you expect the DNA of a chimpanzee to be more like that of a gorilla or an orangutan? Explain your answer.

_____

_____

Lesson 8   Primates

~~~~~~

Use the following diagram that shows several primates to answer the questions that follow.

1. Which primate shares the most traits with humans? What are these traits?

_____

_____

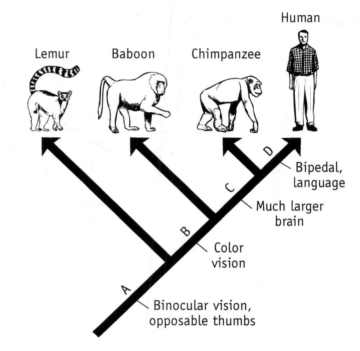

2. What characteristic is used to separate the baboon from the chimpanzee?

_____

_____

3. What letter represents a point where humans and lemurs have the same characteristics?

_____

_____

4. What characteristic do baboons have that lemurs do not have? Explain your answer.

_____

_____

5. If monkeys were included in the diagram above, where would they be placed? Explain your answer.

_____

_____

Lesson 8

Comparing Hemoglobin

The following illustration shows the sequence of amino acids that make up hemoglobin in humans, gorillas, and horses. Only a part of the sequence is shown. An abbreviation is used for each amino acid. Use this illustration to answer the questions that follow.

Human: asp-pro-glu-asn-phen-arg-leu-leu-gly-asn-val-leu-val-csy-val-leu-ala-hist

Gorilla: asp-pro-glu-asn-phen-lys-leu-leu-gly-asn-val-leu-val-csy-val-leu-ala-hist

Horse: asp-pro-glu-asn-phen-arg-leu-leu-gly-asn-val-leu-ala-leu-val-val-ala-arg

1. Do these sequences support the theory that humans are more closely related to gorillas than they are to horses? Explain your answer.

_____

_____

_____

2. Which two organisms are likely to have the most similar DNA? Explain your answer.

_____

_____

_____

3. Cytochrome c is another protein that has been compared in different animals. What would you expect to find if you compared the cytochrome c in humans, gorillas, and horses? Explain your answer.

_____

_____

_____

Lesson 8   Experiment: Extracting DNA

Taking out the DNA from the cells of an organism is a rather simple process, as you can see by doing the following experiment. You will use a liquid detergent to break open pea cells to release the DNA. You will then use meat tenderizer to break down proteins. This will leave the DNA that you can then pick up with a wooden skewer.

What You Need

measuring cup
dried split peas
water
teaspoon
table salt
blender
tablespoon
liquid detergent
narrow glass container
strainer
meat tenderizer
wooden skewer
rubbing alcohol

Procedure

1. Place half a cup of split peas, a cup of cold water, and 1/4 teaspoon of table salt in a blender.

2. Blend on the high setting for 15 seconds. The pea "soup" should be so thick that you cannot see through it. If your "soup" is too thin, add more peas and blend again.

3. Pour the pea "soup" through a strainer and collect the liquid in the measuring cup.

4. Add 2 tablespoons of the liquid detergent. Allow the mixture to stand for 15 minutes.

5. Pour some of the mixture into the glass container.

6. Add a pinch of meat tenderizer.

7. Use the skewer to stir the mixture very gently.

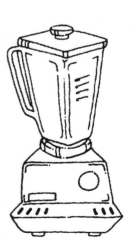

Experiment: Extracting DNA (cont'd.)

8. Tilt the glass container and slowly pour the rubbing alcohol down the side so that it forms a layer on top of the greenish mixture. Pour about the same amount of alcohol as you have greenish mixture.

9. Insert the skewer into the alcohol-pea mixture and gently swirl it.

Results and Analysis

Describe what collects on the skewer.

_____

_____

Conclusion

What conclusion can you draw based on your observations?

_____

_____

_____

_____

_____

Lesson 9 Earth's History and Structure

Earth provides all the resources needed for life. For example, Earth provides the water we drink, the air we breathe, and the food we eat. Any resource that Earth provides and which organisms such as humans use is called a **natural resource**. Natural resources include water, oxygen, minerals, and petroleum. There are two types of natural resources: renewable and nonrenewable.

Renewable and Nonrenewable Resources

A **renewable resource** is a resource that can be replaced at the same rate that it is used. Examples of renewable resources include soil, trees, water, and oxygen. These resources are replaced by natural processes. For example, trees are produced by seeds planted in the soil.

Some renewable resources, such as water, are recycled. The **water cycle** describes the constant movement of water through the environment and living things, and back again. The illustration on the next page summarizes the water cycle.

Key Terms

natural resource—any resource that Earth provides and which organisms use

renewable resource—a resource that can be replaced at the same rate that it is used

water cycle—the processes that constantly move water through the environment and living things

evaporation—the process by which water changes from the liquid state to the gas state (water vapor) when it is heated

respiration—the process by which organisms get and use oxygen and release carbon dioxide and water

transpiration—the process by which water evaporates through openings in plant leaves

condensation—the process during which water changes from the gas state to the liquid state when it loses heat energy

precipitation—any form of water that falls to Earth such as rain, snow, sleet, and hail

nonrenewable resource—a resource that is used or consumed much faster than it is formed

energy resource—a natural resource that can be converted into a form of energy that can do useful work

solar energy—the energy received by Earth from the sun

wind power—the use of wind turbines to generate electrical energy

hydroelectric energy—the electrical energy produced by using falling water

geothermal energy—the energy produced by using the heat within Earth

fossil fuel—an energy resource formed from the remains of animals and plants that lived long ago

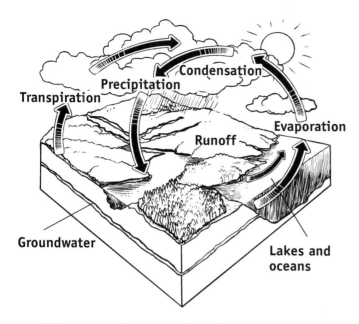

Water enters the atmosphere through three processes: evaporation, respiration, and transpiration. **Evaporation** is the process by which water changes from a liquid to a gas (water vapor) when it is heated. **Respiration** is the process by which organisms get and use oxygen and release carbon dioxide and water. Respiration releases water vapor back into the atmosphere. **Transpiration** is the process by which water evaporates through openings in plant leaves.

Water is returned from the atmosphere through two processes: condensation and precipitation. **Condensation** is the process during which water changes from a gas to a liquid when it loses heat energy. Water vapor in the atmosphere condenses into droplets that make up clouds. When the droplets become heavy enough, they fall as precipitation. **Precipitation** is any form of water that falls to Earth such as rain, snow, sleet, and hail.

Although soil, trees, water, and oxygen are renewable resources, they can be used up before they can be renewed. For example, forests can be cleared to grow crops faster than new forests can grow to replace them. In addition, human activity has affected the recycling of some renewable resources. Filling in lakes and streams to construct roads and houses reduces the amount of water that can enter the atmosphere through evaporation.

A **nonrenewable resource** is a resource that is used or consumed much faster than it is formed. Examples of nonrenewable resources include coal, petroleum, and natural gas. Once these resources are used up, they are no longer available. When these resources become scarce, then humans will have to find other resources to replace them.

Energy Resources

You rely on energy to run the electrical devices in your home. You may use electricity to run a refrigerator, microwave, radio, or clock. Your home may even require electricity to cook food or heat water. Electricity is produced at a power generating plant, which converts some form of energy to electrical energy. The form of energy used to generate electricity is called an energy resource. An **energy resource** is a natural resource that can be converted into a form of energy that can do useful work.

Renewable Energy Resources

Some energy resources are renewable. Renewable energy sources include solar energy, wind power, hydroelectric energy, and geothermal power.

Solar energy from the sun can be changed into electrical energy with the use of solar cells. You may use a calculator that is powered by solar cells. Large solar panels are mounted on homes and businesses to provide both electrical and heat energy. The disadvantage to solar power is the large expense. The cost of installing a complete solar system can be one-third the cost of a house.

Wind power is possible because of solar energy. Solar energy heats the air unevenly, creating the wind. Wind turbines can generate electrical energy. However, in many areas, the wind is not strong or frequent enough to generate sufficient energy.

Hydroelectric energy is generated by using falling water. Huge dams must be built to trap enough water to generate electrical energy. However, these dams can create erosion problems, affect water quality, and harm aquatic organisms.

Geothermal power comes from the heat within Earth. In some areas, magma heats the groundwater which can become steam. The hot water and steam can be used to generate both electrical energy and heat energy.

Nonrenewable Energy Sources

Most of the energy we use comes from a group of resources known as fossil fuels. A **fossil fuel** is an energy resource formed from the remains of animals and plants that lived long ago. Fossil fuels include petroleum, natural gas, and coal.

Petroleum is a liquid fossil fuel. Petroleum is also known as crude oil, which is separated to make several fossil fuels. These include gasoline, jet fuel, diesel fuel, fuel oil, and kerosene. Natural gas is a gaseous fossil fuel. The components of natural gas that are used as fossil fuels include methane, propane, and butane. Coal is a solid fossil fuel. In the early 1900s, coal was the major source of energy in the United States. Because burning coal produces air pollution, petroleum replaced coal as our major energy source.

Petroleum and natural gas form mainly from the remains of tiny sea organisms. When these organisms die, their remains settle on the ocean floor. Here they are buried to become part of the ocean sediment. This sediment slowly becomes rock. Trapped under the rock for millions of years, the remains eventually become petroleum and natural gas. More rocks gradually form above the rocks that contain the fossil fuels. The pressure from the overlying rocks forces the fossil fuels closer to the surface where they collect in reservoirs. Oil wells are drilled to reach these reservoirs.

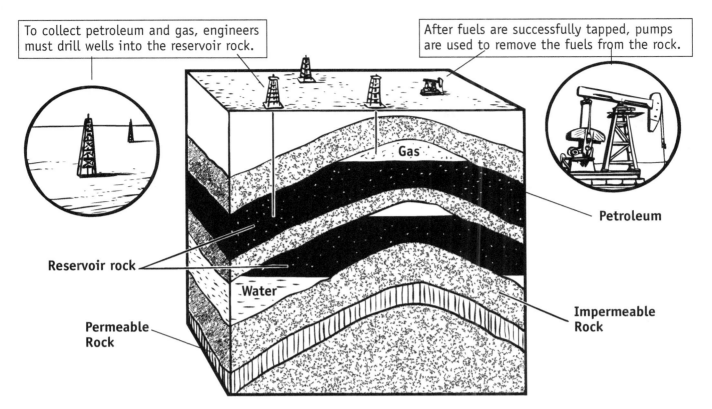

To collect petroleum and gas, engineers must drill wells into the reservoir rock.

After fuels are successfully tapped, pumps are used to remove the fuels from the rock.

Gas

Petroleum

Reservoir rock

Water

Impermeable Rock

Permeable Rock

Coal forms from decayed swamp plants that settle to the bottom where they become part of the sediment. The decayed plants then go through four stages of coal formation: peat, lignite, bituminous coal, and anthracite. At each stage, the percentage of carbon in the material increases. For example, peat is about 60 percent carbon, while anthracite is about 90 percent carbon. The higher the carbon content is, the more cleanly the material burns. The coal that eventually forms is obtained by mining deep beneath Earth's surface.

Energy is released when fossil fuels are burned. For example, burning natural gas may provide the heat energy for the stove in your house. Burning coal in a power plant may generate the electrical energy for your television set. However, fossil fuels are a nonrenewable resource because they take millions of years to form. We are using them much faster than they can be replaced. Therefore, once they are burned, fossil fuels are gone.

Reduce, Reuse, and Recycle

In the meantime, we must conserve our energy resources so that they will last as long as possible.

One of the main ways is to *reduce* what we use. The following pie chart shows how energy is used in the United States.

How Energy Is Used in the United States

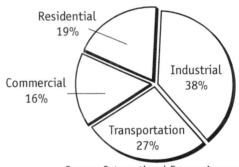

Source: International Energy Agency.

Another way to conserve resources is to *reuse* a product if possible before discarding it. Still another way to conserve resources is to *recycle*. For example, recycling paper reduces the number of trees that must be cut down to make new paper products. Recycling an aluminum can reduces the amount of energy that must be used to extract the aluminum from the ground and make the can. The amount of energy saved by recycling just one aluminum can is enough to power a television for four hours.

Lesson 9   Review

Darken the circle by the best answer.

1. Which term best completes this analogy?

   petroleum : nonrenewable as
   _____ : renewable

   Ⓐ oil   Ⓒ tree
   Ⓑ plastic   Ⓓ gasoline

2. Which process does *not* play a role in the water cycle?

   Ⓐ condensation
   Ⓑ evaporation
   Ⓒ transpiration
   Ⓓ decomposition

3. Which process is an example of using a renewable resource?

   Ⓐ burning wood in a fireplace
   Ⓑ burning propane gas in a barbecue
   Ⓒ burning gasoline in a car
   Ⓓ recycling used oil from a car

4. Which is a renewable energy resource?

   Ⓐ hydroelectric power
   Ⓑ propane
   Ⓒ coal
   Ⓓ gasoline

5. Identify the two energy resources that depend upon the sun.

   Ⓐ geothermal power and wind power
   Ⓑ solar power and nuclear power
   Ⓒ petroleum and coal
   Ⓓ wind power and solar power

6. Which energy resource comes from decayed swamp plants?

   Ⓐ gasoline
   Ⓑ coal
   Ⓒ methane gas
   Ⓓ diesel fuel

7. What are the three *R*s for conserving our energy resources?

   _____

8. Wind energy uses a renewable resource that is free. In addition, wind energy does not cause any pollution. Then why is the use of wind power limited to certain areas?

   _____

   _____

9. How does precipitation depend upon evaporation in the water cycle?

   _____

   _____

Lesson 9   Complete the Sentences

Use the following list of words to complete each sentence. Each word may be used only once.

condensation	nonrenewable resource	transpiration
fossil fuel	renewable resource	water cycle
geothermal energy	respiration	
hydroelectric energy	solar energy	

1. During the process of _____, animals release water into the atmosphere.

2. During the process of _____, plants release water into the atmosphere.

3. _____ is an example of a renewable energy resource that is not produced on Earth.

4. A _____ is an energy resource that formed from the remains of animals and plants that lived long ago.

5. Precipitation plays an important role in the _____.

6. _____ is a renewable energy resource that is generated by Earth's heat.

7. Petroleum is an example of a _____.

8. During _____, water vapor turns into water droplets.

9. _____ is an example of a renewable energy resource that is generated by using falling water.

10. Wood is an example of a _____.

Lesson 9   Drinking Water

Precipitation that falls to Earth can follow several pathways in the water cycle. The precipitation can flow over land into rivers and streams. This is called runoff. Precipitation can also move through pores and other spaces in soil due to gravity. This is called percolation. Percolation replenishes the water table, an area of underground water, which provides fresh water for many homes. The illustration below shows four wells that have been drilled to different depths in the ground. Use this illustration to answer the questions that follow.

1. Which well is *least* likely to be a reliable source of fresh water? Explain your answer.

_____

_____

_____

2. Explain what would happen to the level of the water table following heavy rains. How would this affect which wells might supply fresh water?

_____

_____

_____

3. Would well 4 be able to provide fresh water if a drought occurred? Explain your answer.

_____

_____

4. Which well is most likely to provide fresh water during a drought? Explain your answer.

_____

_____

Lesson 9   Energy Resources

The pie chart below shows where the world gets its energy resources. Use this chart to answer the questions that follow.

1. What are two energy resources that are included in "other energy resources"?

_____

_____

World Usage of Energy Resources

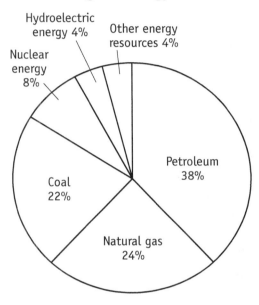

2. What percentage of the energy used in the world comes from a liquid fossil fuel? From a solid fossil fuel?

_____

_____

3. What percentage of the energy used in the world comes from all fossil fuels?

_____

_____

4. What effect would the building of more dams have on the world usage of energy resources?

_____

5. Which energy resource depends upon the use of radioactive materials?

_____

_____

Lesson 9   If It's Saturday, It Must Be Pizza Night!

Read the following passage and then answer the questions.

Could you live for weeks or even months without ever going outside? More than a hundred men eat, sleep, and work in a slender metal tube for months at a time. This metal tube is a nuclear-powered submarine. Nuclear power is the energy resource that is used to keep the submarine operating for months without ever rising to the surface. This power is supplied by a nuclear reactor. Inside this reactor, atoms are broken apart. Each time an atom is broken apart, a tiny amount of matter is changed into energy. This is known as a nuclear reaction. In this type of reaction, an enormous quantity of energy is generated from an extremely tiny amount of matter.

The energy produced by the nuclear reaction is released as heat. This heat turns water into steam within a primary cooling system. The steam is then used to heat water in a secondary cooling system. This steam drives the turbines to provide the energy needed to turn the propellers and generate electricity for the submarine and its crew.

The electricity is used to power all the weapons systems, operate the lights, and provide fresh water for drinking. In addition, the electricity is used to maintain a breathable environment. The air inside a submarine must be constantly purified and replenished with oxygen. A submarine is a closed system and must maintain its own atmosphere.

Electricity is also used to provide entertainment for the crew members, who can watch videos and play games while not on duty. Electricity also provides the energy needed to cook all their meals. Saturday night is traditionally pizza night aboard some nuclear-powered submarines.

1. Describe what happens during a nuclear reaction.

_____

_____

_____

_____

2. Why is a nuclear-powered submarine considered a closed system?

_____

_____

_____

_____

_____

3. Why do you think crew members for a nuclear-powered submarine must be carefully screened before they are accepted for active duty?

_____

_____

_____

_____

_____

www.harcourtschoolsupply.com
© Harcourt Achieve Inc. All rights reserved.

98

Lesson 9, If It's Saturday, It Must Be Pizza Night!
Science 7, SV 9781419034350

Lesson 9

Experiment: Hydroelectric Power

You learned that hydroelectric energy is a renewable resource. A hydroelectric power plant uses falling water to turn a turbine. The turbine generates electricity that is then sent over power lines to homes and businesses, as shown in the illustration.

Notice that water flows from the bottom of the reservoir through a tunnel called a penstock to the turbines. In this experiment, you will learn why water is taken from the bottom of the dam.

Typical Hydroelectric Dam

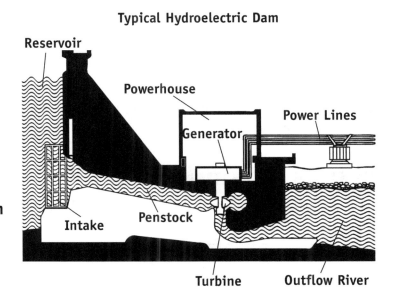

You Will Need

scissors	marker
half gallon paper milk carton, empty and rinsed	finishing nail
	masking tape
ruler	sink

Procedure

1. Cut the top off the milk carton.

2. Starting at one inch from the bottom of the carton, place six marks, each one inch higher than the previous one. The marks should be in the center of one side.

3. Use the nail to poke a tiny hole in the carton at each mark. Be sure to make all holes the same size.

4. Use a piece of tape to cover each of the six holes.

5. Mark a line on the carton near the top. Place the carton so that the holes are facing the sink.

6. Fill the carton with water to the line at the top.

7. Remove the tape from the top hole. Measure how far the water streams out of the hole.

8. Tape the hole again.

Experiment: Hydroelectric Power (cont'd.)

9. Repeat steps 6–8, but this time remove the tape over the second hole from the top.

10. Repeat steps 6–8, but each time remove the tape from the hole beneath the previous one you opened.

11. Experiment to see if opening more than one hole at a time affects how far the water streams out of the carton.

Results and Analysis

1. Describe what happened when you opened different holes in the milk carton.

_____

_____

_____

2. The greater the pressure on the water in the carton, the farther the water will travel. Where in the milk carton is the water under the greatest pressure? Explain your answer.

_____

_____

_____

3. Explain why a hydroelectric power plant is always built at the base of a dam.

_____

_____

_____

Conclusion

What conclusion can you draw based on the results of your experiment?

_____

_____

_____

Lesson 10 Earth in the Solar System

Over 1800 years ago, a Greek named Claudius Ptolemy wrote a book that combined everything that people knew about our solar system at that time. Ptolemy wrote that the universe consisted of just the sun, the moon, and the planets. Stars were believed to be the edge of the universe. Ptolemy did some mathematical calculations and developed the idea that Earth was at the center of our solar system. In 1543, this concept of our solar system was totally changed. That year, a Polish scientist named Nicolas Copernicus published a book in which he said that the sun was the center of our solar system. Copernicus said that all the planets, including Earth, orbited the sun.

Earth's Formation

Scientists think that our solar system formed about 5 billion years ago from a cloud of gases and dust particles known as the **solar nebula**. As the nebula slowly collapsed, the gases and particles began to collide with one another. They slowly formed small bodies the size of golf balls. These bodies continued to collide. Some broke apart. Others clumped together

Key Terms

solar nebula—the cloud of gases and dust particles that formed our solar system

planetesimal—an object in space that continues to grow to form a planet

gravity—the force of attraction between two objects because of their masses

density—the ratio of a substance's mass to its volume

crust—the thin, outermost layer of Earth

mantle—Earth's middle layer found between the crust and the core

magma—hot, liquid rock

lava—magma that flows to Earth's surface

core—the central part of Earth

atmosphere—the mixture of gases that surrounds Earth

photosynthesis—the process by which organisms make food using energy from the sun and carbon dioxide

ozone layer—the layer of gases in the upper atmosphere that blocks most of the sun's ultraviolet radiation from reaching Earth

atmospheric pressure—the measure of the force with which the gases in the atmosphere push on a surface

convection cell—a large circular pattern in which air travels

wind—the movement of air caused by differences in air pressure

rotation—the spin of an object such as Earth on its axis

air mass—a large body of air where the temperature and moisture content are similar throughout

front—the area where two air masses meet

to form larger bodies. The largest bodies became small planets, called **planetesimals**. Scientists think that Earth formed within the first 10 million years of the collapse of the solar nebula.

Two factors played an important role in Earth's formation. One factor was heat. Intense heat was generated as planetesimals continued to collide with the young planet. Materials that collected as Earth formed also released heat. The temperature of Earth's interior continued to rise. The intense heat melted the rocky materials that had collected in the interior.

The second factor that helped form Earth was gravity. **Gravity** is the force of attraction between two objects because of their masses. The more mass the objects have, the stronger the force of gravity is between them. Also the closer the objects are, the stronger is the force of gravity between them. As Earth formed and got more massive, gravity crushed the rocky materials at its center. As a result, Earth became rounder.

Earth's Layers

As rocks were crushed and melted in Earth's interior, our planet formed distinct layers. These layers formed as the elements in the rocky materials began to separate. These elements separated because of differences in their densities. **Density** is the ratio of a substance's mass to its volume. Some elements are denser than others because they have more mass in the same volume.

As rocks melted, denser elements such as iron and nickel sank to the center of Earth. Less dense elements floated toward the surface. Elements with densities between these two extremes collected in the middle. As a result, three layers formed.

The **crust** is the thin, outermost layer of Earth. The crust is made of rocks that contain elements with low densities such as silicon, oxygen, and aluminum. The crust ranges between 3 miles to 60 miles thick. It makes up only about 1 percent of Earth's mass. The deepest humans have ever drilled into the crust is about 10 miles.

Below the crust is the **mantle**. The mantle is much thicker than the crust and makes up about 67 percent of Earth's mass. It is about 1860 miles thick and contains mostly iron, magnesium, aluminum, and silicon. The upper part of the mantle is solid, but tremendous heat and pressure make the lower mantle act more like a thick liquid. This thick liquid is called **magma**.

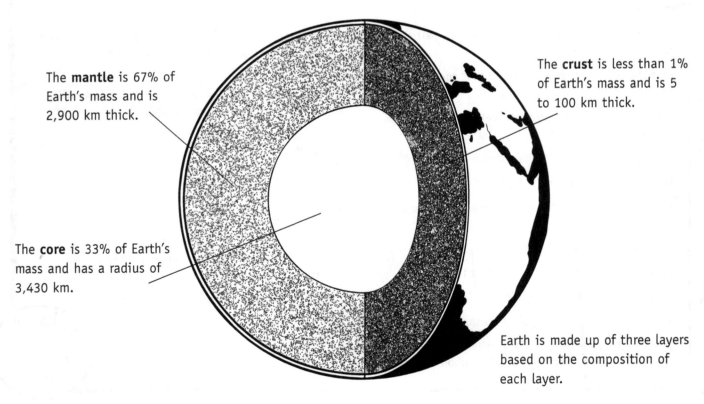

The **mantle** is 67% of Earth's mass and is 2,900 km thick.

The **crust** is less than 1% of Earth's mass and is 5 to 100 km thick.

The **core** is 33% of Earth's mass and has a radius of 3,430 km.

Earth is made up of three layers based on the composition of each layer.

Lesson 10, Earth in the Solar System
Science 7, SV 9781419034350

Because no one has ever seen the mantle, scientists study its composition from observations made on Earth's surface. In some places, magma from the mantle rises to the surface. When a volcano erupts, magma may flow onto Earth's surface. Magma that flows onto Earth's surface is called **lava**. Lava can also rise to the surface from fissures, or cracks, in Earth's crust.

The innermost layer of Earth is called the **core**. It has a radius of about 2200 miles and makes up about 33 percent of Earth's mass. The core is mostly iron, with a little bit of nickel. Unlike the crust and mantle, the core contains almost no oxygen, silicon, aluminum, or magnesium.

The outer part of the core is liquid, but enormous pressures keep the inner part solid. At the center of the core, the temperature is over 10,800°F. The pressure inside the core is four million times greater than at the surface.

The Atmosphere

The **atmosphere** is a mixture of gases that surrounds Earth. Today, the atmosphere is 78 percent nitrogen, 21 percent oxygen, and about 1 percent argon, with traces of other gases such as carbon dioxide. This is very different from Earth's atmosphere when the planet first formed. Scientists think that the early atmosphere was composed mostly of carbon dioxide and water vapor. These gases came from the steamy mixture given off by the molten rocks.

As Earth's layers began to form, the planet changed in other ways. Land masses began to take shape. This was often a violent process accompanied by earthquakes and volcanic eruptions. As volcanoes erupted, they released gases into the atmosphere. These gases included chlorine, methane, ammonia, and water vapor.

Notice that oxygen was not among the gases thought to have been present in Earth's early atmosphere. The first life-forms were very simple and did not need oxygen to live. However, scientists think that these first life-forms slowly changed or evolved. They evolved into organisms that carry out photosynthesis. **Photosynthesis** is the process by which organisms make food using energy from the sun and carbon dioxide. Photosynthesis also releases oxygen into the atmosphere. As a result of photosynthesis, Earth's atmosphere was drastically changed. Over many millions of years, photosynthesis added oxygen to the atmosphere.

Some of this oxygen formed the ozone layer in the upper atmosphere. The **ozone layer** blocks most of the sun's ultraviolet radiation from reaching Earth's surface. Some radiation from the sun does reach Earth, where it plays a role in shaping the weather.

Atmospheric Pressure and Winds

Gravity pulls the gases in the atmosphere toward Earth. This creates atmospheric pressure. **Atmospheric pressure**, or air pressure, is the measure of the force with which the gases in the atmosphere push on a surface. Atmospheric pressure is measured with a barometer. Air pressure decreases with altitude. In other words, air pressure is lower at the top of a mountain than at sea level.

Air pressure is also affected by the unequal heating of Earth. More ultraviolet light directly strikes the equator than other places on Earth. As a result, the air is warmer at the equator. Warmer air is also less dense than cooler air. The warm, less dense air rises and creates an area of low pressure. This rising air flows toward the poles. At the poles, the air is colder and denser than the surrounding air. The cold, denser air sinks and creates an area of high pressure around the poles.

The colder, denser air that sinks at the poles then flows toward the equator. As it does, it warms up and then rises again. As a result, the air travels in many large circular patterns called **convection cells**. These convection cells create wind. **Wind** is the movement of air caused by differences in air pressure.

Winds usually do not travel in a north-south direction between the equator and the poles. Rather they curve to the east and west. This is caused by Earth's **rotation**, or the spin of the planet on its axis. Earth spins in a counterclockwise direction. This causes winds traveling north to curve to the east and winds traveling south to curve to the west. The following illustration shows Earth's major wind patterns caused by differences in air pressure and its rotation.

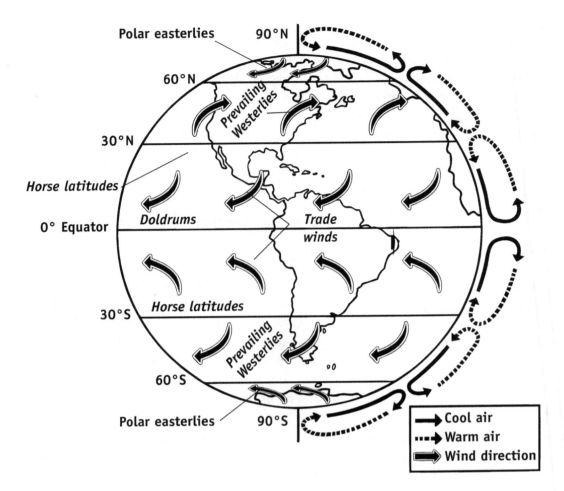

Cool air
Warm air
Wind direction

Air Masses and Weather

Winds cause air masses to move. An **air mass** is a large body of air where the temperature and moisture content are similar throughout. There are many types of air masses. However, all of them can be classified as either a cold air mass or a warm air mass. A cold air mass forms over northern Canada and brings winter weather to the United States. A warm air mass forms over the Gulf of Mexico and brings summer weather to the United States.

The boundary between two types of air masses is called a **front**. A *cold front* forms where cold air moves under warm air. This pushes up the warm air. A *warm front* forms where warm air moves over cold air. The warm air gradually replaces the cold air. In some cases, the warm air does not have enough force to replace the cold air. In this case, a *stationary front*

develops. A stationary front often brings several days of cloudy, wet weather. The illustrations on page 105 show the different types of fronts.

A cloud is a collection of billions of tiny water droplets or ice crystals. A cloud forms as warm air rises and cools. As the air cools, the water vapor in the air changes to a liquid or solid, depending on the temperature. At temperatures above freezing, the water vapor turns into a liquid. Rain may follow. A cloud produces rain when the water droplets become large enough to fall to Earth because of gravity.

At temperatures below freezing, the water vapor turns into ice crystals. Snow may follow. Snow can fall as single ice crystals or can join to form snowflakes. Snowflakes are six-sided crystals that can grow to several inches in size.

Cold Front

Direction of front →

Cold air mass   Warm air mass

Warm Front

Direction of front →

Warm air mass   Cold air mass

Stationary Front

Cold air mass   Warm air mass

Lesson 10, Earth in the Solar System
Science 7, SV 9781419034350

Lesson 10

Review

Darken the circle by the best answer.

1. Air travels in a large circular pattern known as a
   - Ⓐ front.
   - Ⓑ convection cell.
   - Ⓒ solar nebula.
   - Ⓓ rotation.

2. In which layer of Earth are the densest elements located?
   - Ⓐ crust
   - Ⓑ mantle
   - Ⓒ core
   - Ⓓ atmosphere

3. Solar radiation warms the air so that it becomes
   - Ⓐ less dense and rises.
   - Ⓑ less dense and sinks.
   - Ⓒ more dense and rises.
   - Ⓓ more dense and sinks.

4. Which gas is thought to have been missing from Earth's early atmosphere?
   - Ⓐ water vapor
   - Ⓑ carbon dioxide
   - Ⓒ ammonia
   - Ⓓ oxygen

5. Which two factors played an important role in Earth's formation?
   - Ⓐ wind and air pressure
   - Ⓑ heat and gravity
   - Ⓒ solar radiation and convection cells
   - Ⓓ cold fronts and warm fronts

6. Winds do not normally travel in a north/south direction because of Earth's
   - Ⓐ atmospheric pressure.
   - Ⓑ composition.
   - Ⓒ rotation.
   - Ⓓ ozone layer.

7. How do clouds form?

   Billions of water vapor particles that were solidified into ice crystals.

   _____

   _____

   _____

8. How did photosynthesis affect Earth's atmosphere?

It added oxygen into the atmosphere.

9. Why did Earth separate into distinct layers as it was being formed?

Different Materials.

Lesson 10   Velocity in Space

In Lesson 2, you learned that velocity is the speed of a moving object in a particular direction. The diagram below illustrates the velocity of a spacecraft after it has been launched. Orbital velocity is the velocity required to enter in orbit around Earth. Escape velocity is the velocity required to overcome Earth's gravity and travel into space. Use this illustration to answer the questions that follow.

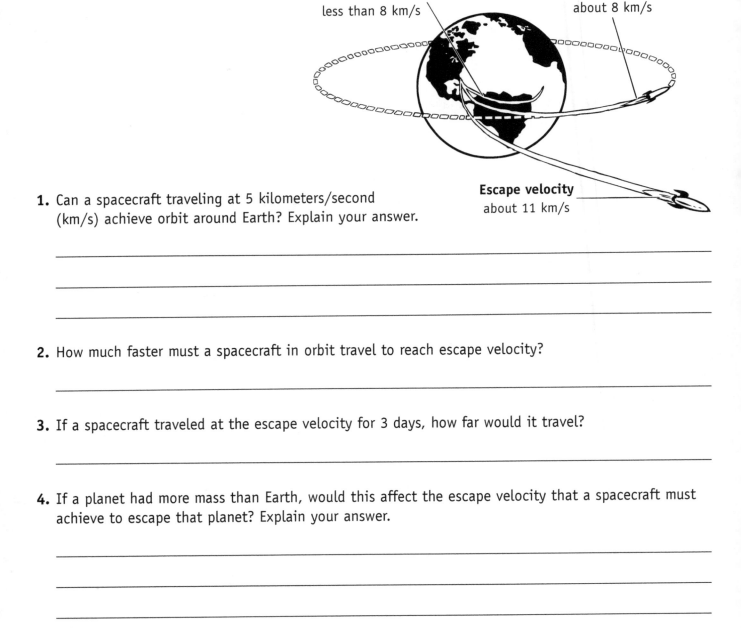

Suborbital velocity
less than 8 km/s

Orbital velocity
about 8 km/s

Escape velocity
about 11 km/s

1. Can a spacecraft traveling at 5 kilometers/second (km/s) achieve orbit around Earth? Explain your answer.

_____

_____

_____

2. How much faster must a spacecraft in orbit travel to reach escape velocity?

_____

3. If a spacecraft traveled at the escape velocity for 3 days, how far would it travel?

_____

4. If a planet had more mass than Earth, would this affect the escape velocity that a spacecraft must achieve to escape that planet? Explain your answer.

_____

_____

_____

Lesson 10   Be a Weather Forecaster

Use the weather map below to answer the questions that follow.

1. Where is warm air moving over cold, denser air? Explain your answer.

   _____

   _____

   _____

2. Where is cold air moving under warm air that is less dense? Explain your answer.

   _____

   _____

   _____

3. Where is the weather likely to be cloudy and rainy for several days? Explain your answer.

   _____

   _____

4. How are the fronts in Seattle and Boston similar? How are they different?

   _____

   _____

Lesson 10   Tornadoes

Read the following passage and then answer the questions.

On March 12, 2006, more than 100 tornadoes were reported in the Midwest. In Missouri, a 20-mile-long path of destruction tore across the state. More than 100 homes were damaged or destroyed. A 19-year-old man was carried more than 1300 feet through the air, setting a record. He was blown from his mobile home to an open field. Amazingly, he lived to tell about it.

About 75 percent of the world's tornadoes occur in the United States. Most of these tornadoes occur in the spring and early summer. During these times of the year, cold, dry air from Canada meets warm, moist air from the south. The wind is moving in two directions where these fronts meet. This causes a layer of air in the middle to spin like a roll of toilet paper. Strong updrafts of air from the ground turn the column into a vertical position. The spinning column of air forms a funnel cloud. The funnel cloud becomes a tornado when it touches the ground.

Most tornadoes last for only a few minutes. But they can cause a lot of damage because of their strong spinning winds. Most tornadoes produce winds between 75 and 120 miles per hour. A violent tornado can have winds of over 300 miles per hour. These strong winds explain why buildings do not explode in a tornado where the air pressure is very low. The winds slam into the buildings, preventing them from blowing apart. Opening the windows to equalize the pressure is a myth. The safest thing to do is to leave the windows alone and seek shelter.

If you are inside, the best place to go is a basement or cellar. Or you can go to a windowless room in the center of the building, such as a bathroom, closet or hallway. If you are outside, lie down in a large, open field or a deep ditch.

1. The safest thing to do if you are caught outdoors during a tornado is to
   (A) stay close to a building.
   (B) stand under a tall tree.
   (C) lie down in a deep ditch.
   (D) run for cover.

2. Weather forecasters will issue a tornado watch if they observe certain conditions. What condition may cause a tornado watch to be issued?
   (A) a rising temperature
   (B) a rising barometer
   (C) the appearance of rain clouds
   (D) the approach of a warm front with a cold front

3. A tornado warning is issued if a tornado has been spotted. What must happen for someone to claim that he or she has spotted a tornado?
   (A) Winds must be blowing in excess of 75 miles per hour.
   (B) A funnel cloud must have touched the ground.
   (C) A building must have been damaged or destroyed.
   (D) A cold front must have recently passed through the area.

Lesson 10

Earth Crossword Puzzle

Across

2. the ratio of mass to volume

5. where you would find the densest elements on Earth

8. hot, liquid rock

10. the most common gas in the atmosphere

12. cloud of gases and dust particles

13. device used to measure air pressure

15. Earth's spin

Down

1. what warm air does

3. what Earth once was

4. what photosynthesis adds to the atmosphere

5. the thinnest layer of Earth

6. what protects us from harmful ultraviolet rays

7. a collection of billions of water droplets

8. Earth's middle layer

9. the type of front that often brings cloudy, wet weather

11. the force of attraction between two objects due to their masses

14. the movement of air

Lesson 10   Experiment: Forecasting the Weather

You have probably heard a weather forecaster report that the barometric pressure is rising or falling. A rising barometer indicates that fair weather is approaching. In contrast, a falling barometer indicates the approach of foul weather. In this experiment, you will make your own barometer to use in forecasting the weather.

You Will Need

plastic wrap
large, empty coffee can
rubber band
straight pin
straw
tape
index card
flat wall surface
table
pencil

Procedure

1. Stretch the plastic wrap over the opening of the can. Use the rubber band to hold the plastic wrap in place.

2. Push the pin through the end of the straw.

3. Place the straw on the plastic wrap so that about one-third of it sticks out past the edge of the can. Tape the straw to the plastic wrap.

4. Tape the index card to the wall. Place the can on the table so that the pin touches the index card. This is your barometer. Use the pencil to mark the spot where the pin touches the index card. Then move the can about 1 cm to one side.

5. Use your barometer to collect and record information about air pressure during the week. Each day, mark and label the spot on the index card where the pin touches.

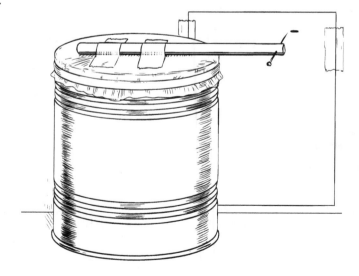

Experiment: Forecasting the Weather (cont'd.)

Results and Analysis

1. What does it mean when the pin moves up?

_____

_____

2. What does it mean when the pin moves down?

_____

_____

Conclusion

What conclusion can you draw based on your observations?

_____

_____

_____

Science Fair Projects

Although it is at the end of the lesson, each experiment in this book should be the beginning for learning something about science. You may have done the experiment titled *The Digestive System* and observed how an enzyme speeds up the rate of a chemical reaction. But you can also experiment to determine if enzymes work best at certain temperatures by using warm and cool solutions. You can also test if the enzyme works on substances other than gelatin such as solid egg white and other protein-rich foods. You can do some research to see how enzymes speed up chemical reactions. Find out what other household products can be used to observe the effect of an enzyme. One possibility includes the use of hydrogen peroxide and potato. In other words, you should be creative, like any good scientist.

Designing an Experiment

If you design your own experiment, be sure that you do so safely and correctly. You must carry out all your work with the supervision of an adult, either your parent or teacher. The adult must help with any procedure that involves a risk. For example, the experiment may require the use of a sharp knife or hot stove. The adult should perform these steps. In addition, you must have an adult review the materials you will use and the procedure you will follow *before* you begin any experiment or science fair project.

Also be sure that your experiment has been designed correctly. Whenever a scientist designs an experiment, he or she always includes a control. A control is set up so that only one factor or variable is present in the experiment. A variable is anything that changes.

You may have done the experiment titled *Comparing Momentums*. The experiment is designed to determine how changes in mass and velocity affect momentum. You changed the mass by using more marbles each time you did the experiment. However, you did not change the height of the ramp so that the velocity was kept constant. As a result, the only variable was the mass. All other factors were kept the same. Therefore, if the momentum increased, then the change in mass must have been responsible.

Choosing a Project

Any experiment in this book can serve as the basis for a science fair project. Usually, doing a science fair project is a bit more involved than carrying out an experiment. Rather than use an experiment in this book as your starting point, you may want to pick your own topic to investigate. If you do, you will have to do some research to learn something about the topic. This research can involve checking the Internet, reading books, and talking to teachers and scientists.

Deciding what to do for a science fair project is often the hardest part of the project. If you have trouble choosing a project, then here are some ideas from each lesson in this book. These ideas will get you started. However, you will have to obtain more information to carry out the project. You can get this information from the Internet, the library, or your teachers. You can also check companies that sell to individuals for items that can help you with your project.

Lesson 1 Properties and Changes of Properties in Matter

- **Atomic Models**—Make a model to show the structure of an atom. Make models of various elements to show how they differ from one another. Explain how electrons travel around the nucleus in terms of energy levels and explain how they are described in terms of quantum numbers.

- **Mixtures**—Prepare a mixture and show how each component can be separated by physical means. You may want to show how fractional distillation is used to separate the various components in petroleum, which is a mixture.
- **Compounds**—Compounds can be classified as either ionic or covalent. For example, table salt is an ionic compound, while sugar is a covalent compound. Demonstrate the differences in their properties such as their melting points and their ability to conduct electricity when dissolved in water. Explain how each compound is formed from their elements.

Lesson 2 Motions and Forces

- **Forces**—Demonstrate how an object will move only if an unbalanced force is applied. Measure the forces that are applied to an object. To measure the force, you will need to construct a device from rubber bands and a ruler.
- **Acceleration**—Prove that all objects have the same acceleration due to gravity. You will have to time how long it takes for objects of different masses to fall from a considerable height. You will also have to consider the factor of air resistance.
- **The Laws of Motion**—Sir Isaac Newton described the relationship between force and the motion of an object with three laws. Demonstrate each of his laws. Explain how friction affects his first law. Demonstrate how mass and force affect acceleration according to his second law. Provide examples of his third law.

Lesson 3 Transfer of Energy

- **Global Warming**—Construct a model to show how greenhouse gases trap solar energy. Include data on changes in average global

temperature and carbon dioxide levels for the past 50 years.

- **Color**—Demonstrate the difference between color addition and color subtraction. Explain how color addition is used to produce an image on a television screen. Explain how pigments are made by color subtraction.
- **Reflection**—Demonstrate the difference between a concave mirror and a convex mirror. Include ray diagrams to show how both types of mirrors produce an image. Provide practical uses for each type of mirror. Do the same for a concave lens and a convex lens.

Lesson 4 Structure and Function in Living Systems

- **Lung Capacity**—Construct a device that measures lung capacity, including vital capacity and tidal volume. A simple device can be constructed from a balloon and ruler. However, try to build a more accurate method of measuring lung capacity. Check with a medical professional for information about the use of spirometers.
- **Heart Rate**—Use a small organism known as daphnia to see how its heartbeat rate changes as the temperature is raised and lowered. You will need to observe the daphnia under a microscope for at least 30 seconds to obtain accurate measurements.
- **Respiration**—Measure the amount of carbon dioxide a person gives off. The only chemical you need is phenol red indicator. Test different people both before and after they exercise. Prepare a bar graph of your findings.

Lesson 5 Reproduction and Heredity

- **DNA**—The hereditary information is stored in the chromosomes within a molecule called DNA. Use a detergent to extract or take out the DNA from various cells including spinach, broccoli, and chicken liver. Experiment to find out which detergent works best.

- **Fruit Flies**—Much of our knowledge about genetics was initially obtained from studies involving fruit flies known as *Drosophila melanogaster*. Use this organism to demonstrate how a trait is inherited. You can select a trait such as eye color, which follows a pattern of inheritance called sex-linkage.
- **Nature versus Nurture**—Identical twins have been used in scientific studies to evaluate the role of genetics and the environment on intelligence, behavior, and personal preferences. Research what information has been obtained and prepare a report of your findings.

Lesson 6 Regulation and Behavior

- **Homeostasis**—Use an organism known as paramecium to demonstrate how its contractile vacuole maintains homeostasis. The rate at which the vacuole expels water will change depending on the water concentration in its environment. Record the time it takes for the vacuole to fill and then expel water under different conditions. This project will require patient observations with a microscope.
- **Reflex Behavior**—This type of behavior is important to homeostasis but does not involve the brain. An example of a reflex behavior occurs when a person steps on a sharp object. Select a reflex behavior such as having a person press a switch after hearing a sound. Find out if reflex time is affected by a factor such as age, time of day, or the surroundings.
- **Negative Feedback**—Construct a model to show how negative feedback operates in homeostasis. You can take apart a thermostat that uses a mercury switch. Be sure to work with adult supervision at all times as mercury is a toxic substance. The mercury in a thermostat is contained in a sealed glass chamber. Be careful not to break the glass.

Lesson 7 Populations and Ecosystems

- **Eutrophication**—Organisms need nutrients to survive. However, too many nutrients can cause problems. The process by which an ecosystem receives too many nutrients, such as nitrates, is called eutrophication. Demonstrate the effect of eutrophication by adding fertilizer to pond water and see how the organisms are affected.
- **Coral Reefs**—One type of marine ecosystem is a coral reef, which is found in warm, shallow seas. Investigate how a tiny organism known as a coral polyp can build such a massive structure as a reef. Use a microscope to study the structure and behavior of this organism.
- **Predators**—In a forest biome, an owl is a predator. Use owl pellets to identify an owl's prey. These pellets contain undigested materials from an owl's diet. Resources will be needed to identify the source of the remains that include bone fragments and hair.

Lesson 8 Diversity and Adaptations of Organisms

- **Cladograms**—The evolutionary history of different species is sometimes illustrated with a cladogram. Prepare one or more cladograms to show evolutionary relationships. You will have to check the various styles that are used to draw a cladogram. Be sure to use one that is easy to follow.
- **Natural Selection**—Charles Darwin developed the theory of natural selection to explain how evolution occurs. You can either report on an example of natural selection such as the peppered moth or carry out experiments showing how resistance to antibiotics can evolve in bacteria. You will have to learn how to culture bacteria and take special precautions to prevent any contact with the bacteria.

- **Biodiversity**—Use a Berlese funnel to measure biodiversity. This device is used to isolate the tiny organisms that live in the soil and leaf litter on the ground. You can make a Berlese funnel from an empty soda bottle or plastic milk container.

Lesson 9 Earth's History and Structure

- **Transpiration**—Show how light and temperature affect the rate of transpiration. A device called a photometer is used to measure how much water a plant loses under different conditions.
- **Wind Power**—Build a wind turbine. You can build one to operate outdoors or one that works on the wind from a fan. You can also build it so that it lights up a small bulb or generates power output that can be measured on a meter.
- **Hydroelectric Power**—Build a device called a water wheel that uses running water from a faucet to perform some task. Include information on the history of water wheels.

Lesson 10 Earth in the Solar System

- **Earth's Atmosphere**—Carry out an experiment to show that oxygen makes up about 21% of the atmosphere. One way is to use plain steel wool and allow it to rust. Oxygen forms rust in a chemical process called oxidation.
- **Convection**—The transfer of heat energy by the circulation of air is called convection. Build a working model to show how convection operates and how it could move air in a circular pattern.

- **Photosynthesis**—Determine how temperature and light intensity affect how much oxygen is released by plants during photosynthesis. You can use a freshwater plant called elodea that gives off oxygen bubbles while it carries out photosynthesis. Try to develop some way of measuring the volume of oxygen that is produced.

Presenting Your Project

Students usually present their projects in the form of a three-sided display. This display should include all the important information about your project. The l eft side of the display can include any background information you obtained from the Internet, books, or people. You can also place the purpose and procedure of your project on this side.

The center panel on your display should include the title of your project, your name, and grade at the top. All your results should be shown on this center panel. Do not display your results simply by showing what you wrote. Rather try to present them in a more appealing manner. Include photographs, drawings, graphs, and any other visual materials that will help show what you found.

The right side of the display usually includes your conclusion and explanation. Your display will also be more impressive if you include the setup you used in your project or any models that you built. These items are usually displayed on the tabletop in front of the display.

When it is time to present your project, take your time in explaining what you did. Start with the information displayed on the left panel, then move on to the center panel, and then finally review what is shown on the right hand panel. Be sure to impress your listener with what you learned and how much fun you had while doing your science fair project.

Glossary

absorption—the process that occurs when the energy carried by light waves is transferred to the particles of matter (p. 30)

acceleration—the rate at which velocity changes (p. 19)

adaptation—a trait or behavior that increases an organism's chances of survival (p. 67)

air mass—a large body of air where the temperature and moisture content are similar throughout (p. 101)

air resistance—the force that opposes the motion of objects moving through the air (p. 19)

allele—the different forms of the same gene (p. 49)

alveolus—a tiny air sac in the lungs (p. 40)

artery—a vessel that carries blood from the heart to all parts of the body (p. 40)

atmosphere—the mixture of gases that surrounds Earth (p. 101)

atmospheric pressure—the measure of the force with which the gases in the atmosphere push on a surface (p. 101)

atom—the basic building block of matter; the smallest unit of an element that maintains the properties of that element (p. 7)

atomic number—the number of protons an element has (p. 7)

atrium—an upper chamber of the heart (p. 40)

biodiversity—the variety and complexity of life that exists on Earth (p. 78)

biome—a region that contains groups of similar ecosystems and climates (p. 67)

bipedalism—the ability to walk upright (p. 78)

bronchus—one of the two branches of the trachea that leads to the lungs (p. 40)

capillary—a blood vessel through which substances such as oxygen pass (p. 40)

cardiac muscle—the type of muscle that makes up the walls of the heart (p. 40)

cartilage—the soft tissue that prevents bones from rubbing against each other (p. 40)

cell—the smallest unit of an organism that can perform all life processes (p. 40)

cerebellum—the part of the brain that coordinates muscle action (p. 59)

cerebrum—the part of the brain that controls voluntary responses and functions in memory and reasoning (p. 59)

chemical formula—a shorthand method that uses the chemical symbols of elements and numbers to represent a compound (p. 7)

community—the different populations that live in the same place (p. 67)

compound—a substance that is made from two or more elements that are chemically combined or bonded (p. 7)

condensation—the process during which water changes from the gas state to the liquid state when it loses heat energy (p. 90)

convection cell—a large circular pattern in which air travels (p. 101)

core—the central part of Earth (p. 101)

crust—the thin, outermost layer of Earth (p. 101)

density—the ratio of a substance's mass to its volume (p. 101)

deoxyribonucleic acid (DNA)—a chemical compound that stores hereditary information (p. 78)

diaphragm—the muscle that controls breathing (p. 40)

dominant trait—a trait that appears in the first generation of parents that have different traits (p. 49)

ecosystem—all the organisms within a community and the nonliving things with which they interact (p. 67)

electromagnetic wave—a wave that can travel through empty space or matter (p. 30)

electron—a particle with a negative charge that moves around the nucleus of an atom (p. 7)

element—a substance that cannot be easily changed into another substance (p. 7)

embryo—an early stage of development of a plant or animal (p. 78)

endocrine system—the organ system that secretes hormones to regulate body functions (p. 59)

energy—the ability to do work (p. 30)

energy resource—a natural resource that can be converted into a form of energy that can do useful work (p. 90)

epiglottis—a tiny flap that covers the trachea (p. 40)

esophagus—a muscular tube that connects the mouth to the stomach (p. 40)

evaporation—the process through which water changes from the liquid state to the gas state (water vapor) when it is heated (p. 90)

force—a push or a pull (p. 19)

fossil fuel—an energy resource formed from the remains of animals and plants that lived long ago (p. 90)

front—the area where two air masses meet (p. 101)

gene—a segment of a chromosome that determines a particular trait (p. 49)

genetics—the field of science that investigates how traits are passed from parents to offspring (p. 49)

genotype—the genetic makeup of an organism (p. 49)

geothermal energy—the energy produced by using the heat within Earth (p. 90)

global warming—the warming of Earth caused by the atmosphere's trapping of light waves from the sun (p. 30)

glucagon—a hormone that raises the blood sugar level (p. 59)

gravity—the force of attraction between two objects because of their masses (p. 101)

group—a column of elements in the periodic table (p. 7)

hemoglobin—a substance that carries oxygen in the red blood cells (p. 40)

heredity—the passing of traits from parents to offspring (p. 49)

heterozygous—the situation where the two alleles for a gene are different (p. 49)

homeostasis—the maintenance of a constant internal environment despite changes in the external environment (p. 59)

hominid—a primate that walks upright (p. 78)

homologous features—similar features that arose in a common ancestor but perform different functions in different organisms (p. 78)

homozygous—the situation where both alleles for a gene are identical (p. 49)

hormone—a chemical messenger that is made in one part of the body that causes a change in another part of the body (p. 59)

hydroelectric energy—the electrical energy produced by using falling water (p. 90)

inertia—the tendency of an object to resist a change in motion (p. 19)

insulin—a hormone that lowers the blood sugar level (p. 59)

joint—the place where two bones meet (p. 40)

larynx—the voice box (p. 40)

lava—magma that flows to Earth's surface (p. 101)

law of conservation of momentum—the law that states any time objects collide, the total amount of momentum stays the same (p. 19)

ligament—the tissue that connects two bones at a joint (p. 40)

magma—hot, liquid rock (p. 101)

mantle—Earth's middle layer found between the crust and core (p. 101)

mass—the amount of matter in an object (p. 7)

matter—anything that has both volume and mass (p. 7)

medulla—the part of the brain that controls involuntary responses (p. 59)

mixture—a blend of two or more substances, each of which retains its own identity (p. 7)

momentum—the quantity defined as the product of the mass and velocity of an object (p. 19)

motion—the change in position of an object over time with respect to a reference point (p. 19)

natural resource—any resource that Earth provides and which organisms use (p. 90)

negative feedback—a system where a movement in one direction triggers a response in the opposite direction (p. 59)

net force—the combination of all the forces acting on an object (p. 19)

neutron—a neutral particle located in the nucleus of an atom (p. 7)

newton—the unit for force and weight (p. 19)

nonrenewable resource—a resource that is used or consumed much faster than it is formed (p. 90)

nucleus—the central part of an atom made up of protons and neutrons (p. 7)

organ—a group of tissues that work together for a specific job (p. 40)

organ system—a group of organs that work together for a specific job (p. 40)

organism—a living thing (p. 40)

ozone layer—the layer of gases in the upper atmosphere that blocks most of the sun's ultraviolet radiation from reaching Earth (p. 101)

period—a row of elements in the periodic table (p. 7)

periodic table—an arrangement of the elements so that certain similarities appear at regular intervals (p. 7)

permafrost—a layer of permanently frozen soil under the surface (p. 67)

pharynx—a passageway for both food and air (p. 40)

phenotype—the appearance of an organism (p. 49)

photosynthesis—the process by which organisms make food using energy from the sun and carbon dioxide (p. 101)

planetesimal—an object in space that continues to grow to form a planet (p. 101)

population—all the members of the same species that live in the same place (p. 67)

precipitation—any form of water that falls to Earth such as rain, snow, sleet, and hail (p. 90)

primate—a mammal with an opposable thumb and three-dimensional vision (p. 78)

proton—a particle with a positive charge located in the nucleus of an atom (p. 7)

Punnett square—a grid to organize all the possible combinations of offspring (p. 49)

radiation—the transfer of energy as electromagnetic waves (p. 30)

recessive trait—a trait that does not appear in the first generation of parents that have different traits (p. 49)

reflection—the bouncing of light waves off the surface of an object (p. 30)

refraction—the bending of light as it passes from one type of matter to another (p. 30)

renewable resource—a resource that can be replaced at the same rate that it is used (p. 90)

respiration—the process by which organisms get and use oxygen and release carbon dioxide and water (p. 90)

rotation—the spin of an object such as Earth on its axis (p. 101)

scattering—the change in the direction of light waves that collide and bounce off particles (p. 30)

skeletal muscle—a voluntary muscle that is responsible for moving a part of the body (p. 40)

smooth muscle—an involuntary muscle found in internal organs (p. 40)

solar energy—the energy received by Earth from the sun (p. 90)

solar nebula—the cloud of gases and dust particles that formed our solar system (p. 101)

species—group of organisms that have common features and can mate with one another (p. 67)

speed—the distance traveled by an object divided by the time it takes to travel that distance (p. 19)

tendon—the tissue that connects a muscle to a bone (p. 40)

terrestrial biome—a land biome (p. 67)

testcross—a genetic cross used to determine the genotype of an organism (p. 49)

tissue—a groups of cells that work together for a specific job (p. 40)

trachea—a passageway that connects the pharynx to the lungs (p. 40)

transpiration—the process through which water evaporates through openings in plant leaves (p. 90)

vein—a vessel that returns blood from all parts of the body to the heart (p. 40)

velocity—the speed of an object in a particular direction (p. 19)

ventricle—a lower chamber of the heart (p. 40)

vestigial structure—a structure that has no known function but likely functioned in some ancestor of modern organisms (p. 78)

volume—the amount of space taken up, or occupied, by an object (p. 7)

water cycle—the processes that constantly move water through the environment and living things (p. 90)

wavelength—the distance from any point on a wave to the next corresponding point on the wave (p. 30)

wind—the movement of air caused by differences in air pressure (p. 101)

wind power—the use of wind turbines to generate electrical energy (p. 90)

Answer Key

Assessment, pp. 5–6
1. C	**2.** B	**3.** D	**4.** B
5. B	**6.** A	**7.** D	**8.** B
9. C	**10.** D	**11.** D	**12.** C
13. C	**14.** A	**15.** A	**16.** D

Unit 1, Lesson 1
Review, pp. 12–13

1. B	**2.** D	**3.** D	**4.** C
5. B	**6.** B	**7.** A	

8. An element is a substance that cannot be easily changed into another substance by ordinary chemical or physical means. A compound consists of two or more elements that are chemically bonded to one another in a fixed ratio. A mixture consists of two or more substances that can be blended in varying proportions.

9. Filter the mixture to trap the sand. Boil the liquid that passes through the filter to evaporate the water. The salt will remain.

Atoms and Elements, p. 14
1. b and e	**2.** d	**3.** f	**4.** g	**5.** j
6. g	**7.** i	**8.** e	**9.** h	**10.** a
11. b	**12.** c	**13.** a	**14.** b, e, and g	

Compounds and Mixtures, p. 15
1. False. A *compound* consists of two or more elements that are bonded to one another.
2. True
3. True
4. False. The properties of a compound *are different from* the properties of the elements that make up the compound.
5. False. Water is a *compound* made of hydrogen and oxygen.
6. True
7. False. A chemical formula can be used to represent a *compound*.

8. False. Air is a *mixture* that consists of several gases.
9. True

Pain Relievers, p. 16
1. salicylic acid, sodium salicylate, acetylsalicylic acid, methyl salicylate
2. carbon, hydrogen, and oxygen
3. Both are used to relieve pain, and both are made from salicylic acid.
4. Mixture. The crushed aspirin and water retain their properties.

Experiment: Separating the Components in a Mixture, p. 18
Results and Analysis

1. pepper	**2.** sand	**3.** salt

Conclusion

The components in a mixture maintain their properties and can be easily separated from one another.

Unit 1, Lesson 2
Review, p. 23

1. A	**2.** D	**3.** C	**4.** A
5. C	**6.** B	**7.** C	

8. Their masses are different, and momentum depends on mass.
9. Only by knowing the velocity of the wind will the pilot know the wind's direction, which affects the movement of the plane.

Speed, Velocity, and Acceleration, p. 24
Answers will vary. However, each circle must contain an idea or concept. Each arrow must be labeled so that the relationship or connection between the two circles is clear and correct.

Motions and Forces Crossword Puzzle, p. 25
Across

2. mass	**6.** newton	**8.** net force
9. inertia	**10.** speed	**11.** momentum

Answer Key cont'd.

Down
1. force **3.** acceleration **4.** conserved
5. direction **7.** velocity **10.** south

Problem Solving, p. 26
1. 2 N upward; the object will move upward
2. 360 km/h
3. positive acceleration because the velocity is increasing over time
4. 135 kg•m/s north
5. 5 m/s^2

Experiment: Comparing Momentums, pp. 28–29
Results and Analysis
1. Data will vary.
2. More marbles increases the momentum by increasing the mass.
3. Adding another book increases the momentum by increasing the velocity.

Conclusion
Increasing either the mass or velocity of a moving object increases its momentum. This is seen as the marbles transfer their momentum to the cup.

Unit 1, Lesson 3
Review, p. 34
1. B **2.** D **3.** C **4.** D
5. A **6.** B **7.** C
8. The sunshades reflect sunlight, preventing it from entering and warming the car.
9. Answers will vary.

Glowing Meat, p. 35
1. They both emit light.
2. Because it emits ultraviolet light, you would not see any light.
3. Over time, the ultraviolet light emitted by a fluorescent bulb can damage the skin and cause cancer.
4. These bacteria indicate that other bacteria, including those that cause food poisoning, are likely to be growing on the meat.

The Speed of Light, p. 36
1. 183.7 seconds or 3.1 minutes
2. 1.3 seconds
3. 479,880,000 miles
4. 0.21 miles per second or 761 miles per hour

Reflection, Refraction, and Absorption, p. 37
1. Because of refraction, the bird must dive at a spot other than where it sees the fish.
2. Light from the clock reflects from the mirror producing an image that is reversed.
3. At night, the dark wall absorbs what little, if any, light is available. Because no light is reflected from its surface, the wall cannot be seen.
4. Plants reflect green light. A plant would look black if placed in red light because the red light would be absorbed. Therefore, no light would be reflected, making the plant appear black.

Experiment: Pouring Light, p. 39
Results and Analysis
1. The light seems to pour out the jar, just like water.
2. The newspaper keeps the light from being transmitted through the glass. All the light must travel through the water in the jar. The water reflects the light, acting like a wall that keeps bouncing the light back and forth.

Conclusion
Light can be reflected in water so that light seems to pour just like water.

Unit 2, Lesson 4
Review, p. 44
1. C **2.** C **3.** A **4.** D
5. C **6.** B **7.** C
8. The epiglottis closes the opening to the trachea.
9. Because a capillary is only one cell thick, substances, such as oxygen, can pass through it easily.

Answer Key cont'd.

Ulcers, p. 45

1. *H. pylori* bacteria, NSAIDs, and smoking
2. People who develop ulcers may already have a problem with their stomach or small intestine, perhaps from excess acids.
3. Antibiotics kill the *H. pylori* bacteria.

The Circulatory System, p. 46

1. lungs
2. to all body parts except the lungs
3. right atrium
4. structures 2 and 8
5. separate the two sides of the heart
6. to show that blood flows in only one direction
7. structures 5, 6, and 7

Experiment: The Digestive System, p. 48

Results and Analysis

1. The gelatin cubes remain unchanged in the water, apple juice, and orange juice. The gelatin cubes are smaller, or even absent, in the meat tenderizer and pineapple juice.
2. Digestion occurred in the meat tenderizer solution and in the pineapple juice.
3. Both meat tenderizer and pineapple juice contain a substance that digests gelatin.

Conclusion

Meat tenderizer and pineapple juice contain a substance that digests gelatin.

Unit 2, Lesson 5

Review, p. 53

1. C   2. B   3. A   4. C   5. B

6. The allele for blond hair must be recessive.
7. Possible answers include one gene can control many traits, one trait can be controlled by many genes, not all genes have a dominant and recessive allele, and the environment plays a role in the traits that appear in an individual.

A Hidden Message, p. 54

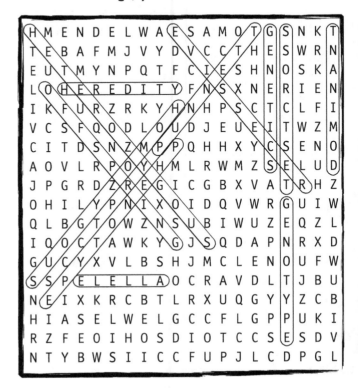

Hidden message: Mendel was a monk.

A Punnett Square, p. 55

1. *TT*
2. All the offspring have tall stems.
3.

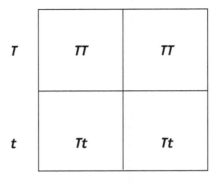

	T	*T*
T	*TT*	*TT*
t	*Tt*	*Tt*

All the offspring are tall.

Answer Key cont'd.

4. *Tt* × *Tt*

5.

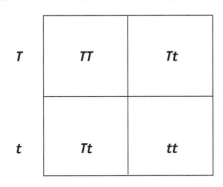

	T	t
T	TT	Tt
t	Tt	tt

Sickle Cell Anemia, p. 56

1. *Ss* (heterozygous); *ss* (person with sickle cell anemia)
2. A person who is heterozygous is protected from malaria.
3.

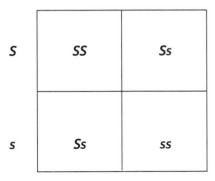

	S	s
S	SS	Ss
s	Ss	ss

The children will include normal (*SS* and *Ss*) and those with sickle cell anemia (*ss*).

Experiment: Making a Pedigree, p. 58
Results and Analysis
1. Answers will vary.
2. A "roller" can be either *TT* or *Tt*.
3. The daughter must have the genotype *Tt*.
Conclusion
Conclusions will vary depending on the pedigree that is constructed.

Unit 2, Lesson 6
Review, p. 63
1. D **2.** B **3.** C **4.** A **5.** C **6.** C
7. The endocrine system plays a role in homeostasis by regulating body functions.
8. If negative feedback were not operating, then blood sugar levels could exceed the normal range by either getting too high or too low.

How Hot Can It Get?, p. 64
1. His body temperature was only 1 degree above normal.
2. Answers will vary. One possibility is that Blagden wanted witnesses to verify his experiment and its results.
3. The steak had been cooked.
4. Answers will vary. One possibility is that Blagden wanted to show that organisms other than humans could also maintain homeostasis.
5. The water would have boiled.

Blood Sugar Levels, p. 65
1. Insulin was being released into the bloodstream. This hormone lowers the blood sugar level.
2. Level dropped from 178 mg/L to 89 mg/L or 89 mg/L in 4 hours (noon to 4 PM) or about 22 mg/L per hour.
3. The level will be below 89 mg/L, perhaps at 78 mg/L.
4. Glucagon would be produced to raise the blood sugar level.

Experiment: Perspiration, p. 66
Results and Analysis
The temperature drops as the alcohol evaporates.
Conclusion
Evaporation of a liquid lowers the temperature and therefore can cool the body.

Answer Key cont'd.

Unit 2, Lesson 7
Review, pp. 71–72

1. C   2. C   3. D   4. A
5. B   6. C   7. A
8. Producing light is an adaptation because it can attract a mate and enable an organism to locate food.
9. The harsh conditions such as freezing temperature and strong winds limit plant life in the tundra.

Biomes of Australia, p. 73

1. D   2. A   3. D   4. B

Deep Below the Surface, p. 74

1. They were surprised to find living things at this depth.
2. A submarine would not be able to withstand the tremendous pressure at this depth.
3. benthic zone
4. An organism must be adapted to survive the enormous pressure, cold temperatures, and lack of light.

Precipitation in a Biome, p. 75

1. about 18 cm
2. The biome could be either a tundra or a desert because of the limited precipitation.
3. The region is most likely a desert because of the temperatures.
4. Answers will vary but can include lizards, snakes, jack rabbits, and mice.

Experiment: Making a Balanced Ecosystem, p. 77
Results and Analysis

1. The fish and snail get their food from the plants.
2. The plants provide the oxygen as a result of photosynthesis.
3. The animals provide the carbon dioxide as a result of respiration.

Conclusion

A balanced ecosystem requires both plants and animals. Plants depend on animals for the carbon dioxide they need for photosynthesis. Animals depend on plants for food and the oxygen they need for respiration.

Unit 2, Lesson 8
Review, pp. 82–83

1. C   2. D   3. B
4. A   5. C   6. A
7. siblings because they are more closely related than cousins
8. Possible answers include comparing skeletal structures, homologous features, vestigial structures, and chemical compounds.

A Common Ancestor, p. 84

1. toothed whales and baleen whales
2. about 70 million years ago
3. camels and llamas
4. hippopotamuses
5. hippopotamuses, toothed whales, and baleen whales

Humans and Apes, p. 85

1. letter A; about 30 million years ago
2. letter D; about 5–7 million years ago
3. chimpanzees
4. humans, chimpanzees, gorillas, and orangutans
5. gorilla; because it is more closely related

Primates, p. 86

1. chimpanzee; binocular vision, opposable thumbs, color vision, large brain
2. brain size
3. point A
4. color vision; Color vision is added as a trait after lemurs separated from the other primates.

Answer Key cont'd.

5. branching off somewhere after point B; Monkeys are primates with opposable thumbs, binocular vision, and color vision.

Comparing Hemoglobin, p. 87

1. yes; Human and gorilla hemoglobin are more similar than either hemoglobin is to the horse's.
2. humans and gorillas because they have the most similar hemoglobin
3. Human and gorilla cytochrome c would be more similar than either is to the horse's.

Experiment: Extracting DNA, p. 89
Results and Analysis
Long threads should collect on the skewer. These threads are DNA molecules.
Conclusion
The DNA can be extracted from the cells of an organism.

Unit 3, Lesson 9
Review, p. 94

1. C   2. D   3. A
4. A   5. D   6. B

7. reduce, reuse, and recycle
8. Wind is steady and powerful enough only in certain areas.
9. Evaporation returns water to the atmosphere where it can condense and then fall as precipitation.

Complete the Sentences, p. 95

1. respiration   2. transpiration
3. Solar energy   4. fossil fuel
5. water cycle   6. Geothermal energy
7. nonrenewable resource   8. condensation
9. Hydroelectric energy   10. renewable resource

Drinking Water, p. 96

1. Well 2 is the least reliable as it is the most shallow and farthest from the water table.

2. The water table would rise. This would mean that well 1 might be able to provide fresh water.
3. If a drought occurs, the water table would drop. If it drops far enough, well 4 may no longer be able to provide fresh water.
4. Well 3 is the most likely as it is the deepest.

Energy Resources, p. 97

1. wind power and solar energy
2. 38% from petroleum; 22% from coal
3. 84%
4. The use of hydroelectric energy would increase.
5. nuclear energy

If It's Saturday, It Must Be Pizza Night!, p. 98

1. Atoms are split, and a small amount of mass is changed into a tremendous quantity of energy.
2. The submarine must supply all its resources, such as clean air and energy, while submerged for long periods of time.
3. Crew members must be selected who can tolerate living in close quarters for long periods of time.

Experiment: Hydroelectric Power, p. 100
Results and Analysis

1. The lower the hole that is opened, the farther the water travels. The water travels farthest when the bottom hole is opened.
2. The water is under the greatest pressure at the bottom because of all the weight of the water above it. This pressure causes the water to travel farthest out the bottom hole.
3. The power plant takes advantage of the high pressure of water at the bottom of a dam. The higher the pressure, the greater the force exerted by the falling water on the turbines. As a result, more electricity is generated.

Conclusion
Water at the base of a dam is under the highest pressure and can create the greatest force to turn the turbines in a hydroelectric power plant.

Answer Key cont'd.

Unit 3, Lesson 10
Review, pp. 106–107

1. B   **2.** C   **3.** A

4. D   **5.** B   **6.** C

7. Water vapor collects in the atmosphere. The cooler temperature causes it to condense into tiny water droplets that collect to form a cloud.

8. Photosynthesis added oxygen gas to Earth's atmosphere.

9. Elements separated because of differences in their densities. The denser elements sank into the interior while the lighter ones floated toward the surface.

Velocity in Space, p. 108

1. No, because it has not reached orbital velocity which is about 8 km/s.

2. about 3 km/s (11 km/s − 8 km/s)

3. 2,851,200 km

4. A planet with more mass would have a stronger gravitational force. Therefore, the escape velocity would be greater on this planet.

Be a Weather Forecaster, p. 109

1. near San Diego where a warm front is indicated on the map

2. near Seattle, Chicago, and Boston where cold fronts are indicated on the map

3. near Tulsa where a stationary front is indicated on the map

4. Both are cold fronts, but they are moving in opposite directions.

Tornadoes, p. 110

1. C   **2.** D   **3.** B

Earth Crossword Puzzle, p. 111
Across

2. density   **5.** core

8. magma   **10.** nitrogen

12. nebula   **13.** barometer

15. rotation

Down

1. rises   **3.** planetesimal

4. oxygen   **5.** crust

6. ozone layer   **7.** cloud

8. mantle   **9.** stationary

11. gravity   **14.** wind

Experiment: Forecasting the Weather, p. 113
Results and Analysis

1. Air pressure is rising and pushing down on the plastic wrap, causing the straw to go up.

2. Air pressure is falling, allowing the air inside the can to push up on the plastic wrap and cause the straw to go down.

Conclusion

A barometer indicates the changes in air pressure. Changes in air pressure indicate changes in the weather.

CPSIA information can be obtained
at www.ICGtesting.com
Printed in the USA
BVHW012145210322
632066BV00012B/356